D0396018

THE FIRE CHEF

FRONTISPIECE *Skewered prawns with grilled mixed vegetables*

David Veljacic

The Fire

CHEF

Fast Grilling and Slow Cooking on the Barbecue

Douglas & McIntyre
Vancouver/Toronto

Copyright © 1999 by David Veljacic

*All rights reserved. No part of this book may be reproduced,
stored in a retrieval system or transmitted in any form or by any
means, without the prior permission of the publisher or, in the
case of photocopying or other reprographic copying, a
licence from* CANCOPY *(Canadian Copyright
Licensing Agency), Toronto, Ontario.*

Douglas & McIntyre Ltd.
201–2323 Quebec Street
Vancouver, British Columbia
V5T 4S7

CANADIAN CATALOGUING IN PUBLICATION DATA

Veljacic, David, 1941–
The fire chef
Includes index.

ISBN 1–55054–697–X

1. Barbecue cookery. I. Title.
TX840.B3V44 1999   641.7′6   C99–910265–6

Editing by Audrey Grescoe
Design by cardigan.com
Photography by John Sherlock with Alistair Bird
Food styling by Jennifer Stamper
Index by Pat Veljacic
Printed and bound in Canada by Friesens
Printed on acid-free paper

The publisher thanks Ozark's Country Meats, South Surrey, B.C.

*The publisher gratefully acknowledges
the support of the Canada Council for the Arts
and of the British Columbia Ministry of Tourism, Small
Business and Culture. The publisher also acknowledges the
financial support of the Government of Canada through the
Book Publishing Industry Development Program.*

To my father and mother, who taught my sister, brother and me to love and appreciate food.

And to Pat, who was supportive, encouraging, patient with my idiosyncrasies and instrumental in producing this book.

I WANT TO THANK all the firefighters who over the past thirty years have tested my recipes – the good, bad and some downright ugly ones.

A special thanks to family and friends who were brave enough to say "yuck" to some of my creations, among them Mike and Lori Antunovic, Jim and Bonny Whiting, Ray and Linda Lam, Fred Roycroft and Betty Duff.

Bob and Sheila Buntain, Steve Burnfield and all the people mentioned above have my gratitude for their assis-

ACKNOWLEDGEMENTS

tance in our fund-raising events, which inspired this book.

I'm grateful, too, to all the chefs, barbecue cooks, cookbook authors and food critics whose help and advice got this book off the ground. And to my fishmonger, butcher and the produce manager at my local supermarket, who filled all my orders, no matter how off-the-wall they may have seemed.

With special thanks to U.S. Air Force Lt. Col. Bob Roberts (retired), who introduced me to the world of barbecue; Jack Perrault, who took me under his wing and helped me learn all about barbecue; the members of the Pacific North West Barbecue Association for electing me their president for the past six years; Paul and Audrey Grescoe, for their friendship and encouragement, and their writing course which revived this project; and Karl Varga, my computer techie. Without his assistance I would still be typing.

–D.V.

I'M A FIREFIGHTER – a captain with the Vancouver Fire and Rescue Service and Vancouver's 1997 Firefighter of the Year. I'm also a barbecue chef. Which makes fire pretty important in my life. But as far as I'm concerned it's food that unites my profession and my avocation. As everyone knows, firemen love to eat. I've been preparing meals in firehall kitchens for more than thirty years – lunches and dinners for the shift, usually eight to twelve people.

Like everyone else, I started barbecuing in my backyard. In the mid-1960s, I discovered the world of competition barbecue and chili cooking. From 1985 when I entered my first chili competition, I've spent many weeks on the road each year, attending about a dozen competitions annually.

Most people seem to have heard about chili cookoffs, but barbecue competitions aren't as well known. Ten years ago the Kansas City Barbecue Society – the leading organization – had about 100 members. Sixty to seventy barbecue events were held in the United States. Now the KCBS has more than 1,500 members. Hundreds

INTRODUCTION

of annual barbecue competitions are held in the U.S. and worldwide – even in Ireland, New Zealand and Thailand. The major North American competitions attract a public attendance from 5,000 to 100,000. The Pacific North West Barbecue Association, which I helped form, holds several sanctioned events each year and has a membership of more than 250.

Barbecue competitions are usually associated with community events and are fund-raisers for charities. The cooks compete for trophies, ribbons and prize money ranging from $2,000 to $25,000. Entering some competitions is just a matter of signing up, but the important ones are by invitation only. I've qualified several times for the World Chili Championship in Terlingua, Texas. (Among 400 competitors, I've placed in the top fifteen.) In 1991 and 1992

I was among twenty-four regional winners invited to cook in the Jack Daniel's Invitational BBQ Cookoff in Lynchburg, Tennessee, placing second in the pork loin category and fourth in the ribs. My wife, Pat, also entered the barbecue world, and we now compete as a team. Together we took a first in the pork shoulder category at a Memphis in May event, which is the first big competition of the season.

For twelve years, Pat and I and some of our friends have put on the Canadian Barbecue and Chili Festival, the largest event of its type on the west coast. It combines the Canadian International Barbecue Championship, the Wild B.C. Salmon BBQ and the B.C. Championship Chili Cookoff. We hold it at the Westminster Quay Public Market in New Westminster, B.C., on the first Saturday in August. Spectators stroll around watching the competing chefs who are cooking chili, salmon, pork ribs, pork butt, chicken and beef brisket. After food has been turned in for judging, the remainder is taken to the main tent where it is sold to the public. In 1998 we had forty judges, fifty to sixty chefs and 31,000 well-fed spectators.

Pat and I really enjoy it when we can barbecue for a few people. For instance, in the summer of 1991 we cooked barbecue beef ribs and chicken halves for athletes, coaches and dignitaries at the opening dinner of the British Columbia Summer Games – feeding 5,000 guests in two and a half hours.

The following year the International Firefighters Convention was held in Vancouver, and we were asked to provide a dinner in Stanley Park. As busloads of hungry people pulled up to the picnic site, we and some helpful friends stood by ready to serve grilled halibut, barbecue pork shoulder, potatoes in parsley butter, assorted vegetables and Memphis-style coleslaw. We started off with an appetizer of prawns and oysters, which we served right out of the frying pan to all 1,800 delegates.

I inherited my interest in cooking from my mother. My preference for seafood – and my expertise in purchasing and preparing it – come from a family that has been in the British Columbia fishing industry for years. My most widely printed recipe – which is featured in this book – is for salmon. I introduced it in 1989 at the Washington State Fair where 107 professional and amateur chefs were competing. The Only Barbecue Salmon took first prize. *The Vancouver Sun* declared it the best recipe of the season that year.

In 1992 I submitted The Only Barbecue Salmon to the annual garlic festival in Gilroy, California. From 800 entries, it and seven others were chosen to be cooked at the competition. This was the first time that the judges had selected a fish recipe. Pat and I flew to California, borrowed a charcoal barbecue (there were no gas units available) and cooked our salmon before a huge crowd sitting outside under a hot sun. Three dishes tied for first place. The tie was broken by counting the number of cloves of garlic in each recipe. Competing against a soup with 150 cloves and a pasta with seventy-five, my salmon, with only eight, placed third.

I designed all the recipes that follow. I've tested them over and over at family functions in our backyard and in the firehalls of Vancouver. They've been approved by firefighters. There's no better recommendation, in my book.

BARBECUE
and Grilling

WHERE'S THE FIRE? What's your hurry?

Those two questions sum up the distinction between barbecue and grilling. And while some people make a fuss about the difference, others have no idea there even is one.

The word *barbecue* comes to us from Spanish explorers who found West Indians cooking meat over a fire on a wooden framework they called a *barbacòa*. For thousands of years, people have been cooking meat over fiery coals and wood or over rocks heated by fire. Stone Age people probably threw an entire carcass over a roaring fire, almost smothering the flames, and then allowed the meat to cook overnight. For centuries people in parts of Asia barbecued in a *kamado*, an efficient, egg-shaped unit that cooks slowly for hours on only a few pounds of charcoal. North American natives used wood grills covered with weeds, branches and leaves, so that fish and game cooked by heat and smoke rather than flame.

These examples share a cooking concept that defines *barbecue* and distinguishes it from *grilling*. Barbecue is a longer process, which can be described as low and slow: low heat (200 to 225°F) and slow cooking over a long period, which may be six to twelve hours. Grilling is about cooking over high heat, searing meat quickly and sitting down to dinner pronto.

When North Americans started backyard barbecuing early in the 1950s, they grilled over charcoal in a simple appliance which is still the most widely used barbecue. The 50-year-old Weber kettle is a versatile piece of equipment, however, capable of both barbecuing and grilling.

Until a few years ago, gas barbecue manufacturers catered to backyard grillers. They raced to produce the barbecue with the highest number of British Thermal Units. The magic number seemed to be 50,000 and most manufacturers reached it. These barbecues could be heated to 600°F with the lid closed. Everyone knew how they worked: you turned a valve, lit the gas, singed the hair on your body, and in eight minutes dinner was ready. You could cook only steaks, chops, skewered meats, chicken pieces, a few seafoods, some vegetables, and the dependable hamburgers and hot dogs. Doing a roast at 50,000 BTU would have been like putting it in an oven on the self-clean phase.

Gradually as the low and slow method of barbecue popular in many restaurants seeped into the backyards of North America, barbecue manufacturers redesigned their equipment. They made units with three or four burners so that temperatures could be controlled by turning on one or more burners. You could grill a steak in ten minutes or slow cook larger cuts of meat or a whole chicken or turkey.

Low and slow barbecue is also called the indirect method. I've devoted a section of *The Fire Chef* to this style of cooking with instructions for both charcoal and gas barbecues. And while I know that for some people barbecue means low and slow cooking, as far as I'm concerned any style of outdoor cooking is barbecue. The distinction I've made in my recipes is between those that are fast grilled and those that are slow cooked, as the title of *The Fire Chef* suggests.

About briquettes and wood

Charcoal briquettes were invented by Henry Ford. Ford's Model T had frames made of hardwood. Scrap pieces were burned down to blackened chunks which Henry's brother-in-law sold under the brand name Kingsford, which is still used today.

There are many brands of briquettes on the market, but most are not 100 per cent hardwood. True charcoal lumps light more easily and burn at a higher temperature. If you cannot find pure hardwood briquettes, search out a brand with the lowest percentage of additives.

I advise against briquettes with built-in starters and against petroleum-based lighter fluids because they taint the food. There are many starters on the market that are not petroleum-based.

With the proper equipment – a charcoal chimney – you can start briquettes using four pages of newspaper. Place the paper below the chimney which is filled with charcoal, light the paper and in less than ten minutes the charcoal is ready to be poured or lifted with tongs into the barbecue.

An electric starter is an option, but not at the beach where you have no source of electricity.

Whatever method is used to start briquettes, they have to burn until they look white or gray before food can be cooked. That generally takes thirty minutes, unless you

(the difference)

hasten the process by using a chimney starter. That is one downside to charcoal barbecuing.

Another is the availability of briquettes, especially for year-round barbecuers, who have to keep a supply on hand because many retailers don't sell them in the winter. Still, charcoal briquettes are the most widely used barbecue fuel, even in areas where gas is an option.

Wood is a second choice. Alder is preferred to barbecue or smoke fish. It creates a light flavour that enhances but doesn't mask the fish. Maple has been used for years in the cold smoking of hams and bacon, but it can provide a good flavour to barbecue food also. Fruitwoods – apple, cherry, plum and pecan – bring good results. They give a light, fruity-smoke flavour to meat.

Other hardwoods – hickory, live oak and mesquite – are widely used by barbecue chefs, who usually choose a local wood. Mesquite is primarily a source of heat. It burns at a high temperature and is suitable for grilling. But on its own, mesquite may give meat a bitter taste. For this reason, other woods are added to produce the smoke flavouring.

Depending on the size of your barbecue, you can burn split logs, wood chunks or wood chips. Chunks and chips are available in many retail stores. For gas or smaller barbecues, you can add aroma and flavouring with packets of wood chips containing herbs and spices, which you place in the barbecue during cooking.

Softwoods, readily available in the Pacific Northwest, are not suitable for barbecues. They are high in resins and will taint food with a bitter taste.

How to Grill the Perfect Steak

Buy 6-ounce filets mignons 1 inch thick. Bring the steaks to room temperature.

Season the steaks with sea salt and tellicherry pepper, a meat seasoning rub or a no-salt seasoning. Let the seasoning sit on the steaks while you preheat the barbecue to medium to high (350 to 400°F).

Put the steaks on the grill directly over the heat. Close the lid. In about a minute, flip the steaks. Close the lid. Continue to turn the steaks every minute for 6 minutes.

By this time the meat will be cooked between rare and medium. If you want a medium steak, grill for 2 minutes more on each side.

Don't use a knife to test for doneness because you will lose the juices. Learn to test by pressing the meat with your finger. When meat is raw, a finger indentation will come up slowly. The indentation will rise faster as the meat progresses through the stages of doneness. Eventually the meat will not hold an indentation, at which point it is overcooked.

my best
MYTH-BUSTING TIPS

As soon as spring has sprung, magazines and newspapers will be filled with barbecue recipes and tips on how to barbecue or grill. Many of these tips will be based on myths. Here's the truth, as I see it.

Tongs or fork: it's a matter of preference.

How many times have you read that you should always use tongs when turning steaks because a fork will puncture the meat and you will lose the juices? The truth is that meat is multicellular. A fork will not pierce enough cells to release a significant amount of juice. In many butcher shops and restaurants, steaks are mechanically tenderized with hundreds of thin knife blades. They remain juicy.

Salt and season meat before you barbecue it.

We're told that salting meat before cooking draws out moisture. If you covered meat with salt and let it sit for weeks – as in the curing of ham – the long, slow process of osmosis would draw moisture from the meat. But salting just before cooking does not reduce juiciness. In fact, seasoning before cooking allows salt and spices to mellow and blend with the meat juices. If you seasoned after cooking, the spices would not have time to meld. They would mask rather than enhance the meat flavours.

Turn a thick steak frequently.

On a barbecue the heat rises from the bottom, driving the steak juices up. If you allow a thick steak (more than three-quarters of an inch) to sit on one side, juices will accumulate on the top. When you turn the steak over, you dump all the juices into the fire. More juice will remain in the steak if you turn it every few minutes. My explanation isn't scientific but I see it as a matter of confusing the juices: they start to rise to the top but you turn the steak, and the juices have to change course. They never get a chance to puddle up near the top.

Drowning meat won't tenderize it.

Acids, such as wine, vinegar and citrus juices, will mask the natural flavour of meat (in some cases this may be desirable) but they have questionable value as tenderizers. Penetration studies of so-called tenderizers, such as papaya or commercial preparations containing plant enzymes, show that natural tenderizing cannot be accomplished. You can't tenderize a tough cut of meat by drowning it. Marinades and tenderizers work only on the meat's surface.

Barbecue Safety Tips

The Gas Barbecue Manufacturers' website recommends dousing flare-ups by pouring on a glass of water or by spraying with water. Open the lid carefully and close it immediately after applying the water.

I keep a mixture of water and baking soda in a spray bottle in case of a flare-up.

Keep your barbecue clean. After every use (after we've eaten that is), I scrape the grid with a wire-bristle brush – the kind used to scrape rust off car fenders. Before the next barbecue session, I turn the flame on high and scrape the grid again.

As soon as you finish cooking, while the food is still on the grid, close the lid and turn off the gas. Shut off the tank before you close the valves. If you do it in the reverse order, there will be gas in the hose which can leak into the barbecue the next time you open the valves.

Have the lid of a gas barbecue completely open when you are igniting it.

Keep small kids away from the barbecue. The outside is hot.

If you use lighter fluid (which I never do), don't pour it over coals that are already lit.

Never the line the bottom of the grill with aluminum foil. It can obstruct proper air flow and doesn't reflect more heat.

Use long-sleeved, heat-proof grill mitts to lift and reposition heavy pieces of meat. I use them once and throw them away because they can't be washed.

Don't criticize the chef when he's holding a long-handled fork.

THE BASICS
of barbecue

Types of Barbecues

Kamados

Used for centuries in Asia and, no doubt, the first slow cookers, they are egg-shaped, ceramic and very heavy. ($250 to $1,700)

Forty-five-gallon drums

One of the first barbecues in North America. Several companies convert them for cooking or you can convert your own. ($25 to $250)

Charcoal barbecues

Can cook the greatest variety of foods. The kettle barbecue and grill is still the most widely used charcoal backyard unit. New models are inset on a stainless steel rolling cart and have propane to start the briquettes. When a spit is installed, charcoal barbecues work well with larger cuts such as roasts and hams. I have seen very large units cook sides of beef. Good brands are Weber, David Klose, New Braunfels, Pitt's and Spitt's (the Cadillac of barbecues) and Binford (a made-in-Calgary copy of Pitt's and Spitt's). ($35 to $600)

Water smokers

These appliances are approximately 18 inches in diameter with a dome-shaped lid. The coals are placed in a large pan in the bottom. A water pan hooks under the grid on which food cooks. Weber and Brinkman are good brands. ($75 to $350)

Propane and natural gas barbecues

As versatile as charcoal barbecues, these units have the added advantage of almost instant heat. Some have three or four independently operating burners so that you can barbecue large cuts of meat on an unfired area of the grid. Rotisseries come with most models. Packets of wood chips can be placed over the fire for a smoky aroma and flavour. Good brands for the backyard are Weber, Ducane, Napoleon (made in Barrie, Ontario), Holland, Brinkman and Grillmaster. ($175 to $5,000)

Barbecue cookers

These appliances have a large barrel-shaped cooking chamber and a separate firebox on one end where charcoal and wood are burned. They cook low and slow at temperatures ranging from 200 to 230°F and are used primarily for large to very large cuts of meat and, of course, beef brisket. Not for steaks, chops or vegetables. Manufacturers are Pitt's and Spitt's, Binford and David Klose. ($500 to $50,000)

Barbecue pellet cookers

Charcoal is the main fuel, but an electric auger feeds wood pellets to the fire to produce the smoke flavour and aroma. Made by Traeger Industries of Oregon. ($350 to $600)

Major Barbecue Events

United States

The American Royal Invitational
   Kansas City, Missouri
Taylor Texas Invitational
   Taylor, Texas
Memphis in May Invitational
   Memphis, Tennessee
Texas Championship Barbecue
   Meridian, Texas
Annual Rib and Chicken Barbecue
   Fresno, California
Pig and Pepper Barbecue Festival
   Carlisle, Maine
California Rib Cookoff
   Clovis, California
Jack Daniel's Invitational
   Lynchburg, Tennessee
The Evergreen State Open
   Winthrop, Washington

Canada

Canadian Barbecue and Chili Festival
   New Westminster, B.C.
Barbecue on the Bow
   Calgary, Alberta

Tools and Fuels

BASTING BRUSHES: long-handled ones with fine, synthetic bristles, especially made for barbecue, are best.

BRIQUETTES: look for a brand with a high percentage of hardwood and a low percentage of additives. Avoid those with built-in starters, which can affect the flavour of food.

CHARCOAL: true charcoal is 100 per cent hardwood. The lumps light more easily and burn at a higher temperature than briquettes with additives.

CHIMNEY STARTER: an inexpensive device in which three to four pounds of charcoal or briquettes can be quickly burned to the ready-to-cook stage before transferring to the barbecue.

DISH MOPS: use with a thin sauce to baste in the early stages of cooking.

FOOD WRAP: good for covering meat while it marinates in a dry spice rub. The best product for keeping cooked foods warm before serving.

GRIDDLE: a solid metal sheet used on gas barbecues to cook pancakes or hashed browns.

GRILL GRIDS or GRILL TOPPERS: perforated, Teflon- or porcelain-coated steel sheets with rims. To keep prawns, shrimp and vegetables from falling into the fire.

HARDWOODS: alder is preferred to barbecue or smoke fish. Apple, cherry, plum and pecan give a light, fruity smoke flavour. Maple, which cold-smokes ham and bacon, is also good for barbecue. Hickory, live oak and mesquite are widely used by barbecue chefs.

HINGED BROILERS: to barbecue fragile or small seafoods, pre-sliced meats and certain vegetables. A short-handled one is easier to manage but a long handle can be kept off the fire.

MESQUITE: burns at a high temperature and is suitable for grilling. Usually used with other woods because on its own it may give a bitter taste.

RIB RACKS: hold ribs on end, allowing you to barbecue more at one time. Similar racks are available for potatoes and chicken.

SKEWERS: wooden ones are the best. To keep them from burning, soak in water for thirty minutes to an hour. As they are inexpensive, I have several packages on hand and always use two skewers per kabob.

SPRAY BOTTLES: fill with fruit juices to flavour food, with water to keep it moist or with water and baking soda (in a four-to-one ratio) to quench flare-ups.

STAINLESS STEEL TRAYS: to transport food to and from the grill. Some people use jelly-roll pans.

STARTERS: come in solid or liquid form. Avoid those that contain petroleum (the white sticks, blocks or squares). Brown or beige solid fuels are petroleum-free. So-called odourless liquid starters may impart a fuel smell to food.

THERMOMETER: a rapid-readout thermometer gives an instant and accurate internal temperature.

TONGS AND FORKS: long-handled ones are best. I use heavy-duty, spring-loaded tongs.

WIRE BRUSHES: to clean the grid. I use the kind sold to scrape rust off metal.

WIRE BASKETS: with deep sides; useful for grilling quantities of vegetables.

Barbecue Essentials

Always preheat the barbecue.

Always barbecue with the lid closed. Open the lid only when basting, mopping or turning foods.

High heat will not always burn off stuck-on food or kill bacteria. Always clean the barbecue before and right after use, which makes the job easier.

Oil the grid with a nonstick cooking spray or paper towel dipped in oil before you heat the barbecue.

Make sure coals are ashen-gray before you begin to cook. This will take approximately thirty minutes in a barbecue or less than ten minutes in a chimney starter.

Soak wood chunks or chips in water for at least one hour before adding them to the fire.

Use wood only during the first two or three hours of the low and slow barbecue process.

Never use softwoods, such as fir and cedar. Because of their high resin content, they will taint food.

Use an instant-read thermometer to check internal temperatures.

To prevent bamboo or wooden skewers from burning, soak them in water for an hour before using.

For kabobs, use two skewers parallel to each other and about a quarter to one-half inch apart to stop vegetables, fruits and some meats from spinning.

When marinating, always use a non-corrosive container, for instance a glass bowl or a plastic bag that zips closed.

A marinade can be used for basting during cooking. Otherwise, it should always be discarded.

Marinated meats should be wiped dry before spices are applied.

Most homemade barbecue sauces can be stored in a sealed container in the refrigerator for up to two weeks.

If a barbecue sauce has a high sugar content (which most do), use it to baste only during the final barbecue or grilling stage.

For grilling, steaks should be at least one inch thick.

Bring any food to be barbecued, roasted or fried to room temperature before cooking.

Never thaw meats, poultry or seafood in a microwave. Always thaw chicken and turkey in the refrigerator.

Season meats at least a half hour before you barbecue, grill or roast.

Barbecue roasts and turkeys should stand for at least twenty minutes before carving.

If you want to make sure that the meat will pull away from rib bones, pierce both sides of each bone several times with a fork before you barbecue, grill or bake.

Parboil large potatoes or solid vegetables prior to grilling or roasting. They will cook more evenly.

Small, slightly yellow limes have a better flavour than the large, dark green ones. To get more juice, poke a small hole in the lime and place it in the microwave oven for twenty to thirty seconds. This is one reason to own a microwave.

Ingredients, SPICE RUBS, Marinades & SAUCES

My Favourite Ingredients

I use the following herbs, spices and food products in my spice rubs or in my cooking. Many are available in supermarkets or specialty food shops. Addresses for mail-order products are on page 176.

BALEINE SEA SALT: one of the highest grades; produced by natural evaporation; available in fine and coarse crystals.

CONIMEX SAMBAL OELEK: a hot pepper sauce used in Indonesian cuisine. Can be used as a jerk sauce with meats and poultry.

GEBHARDT CHILI POWDER: one of the finest chili powder blends.

MELINDA'S XXXTRA HOT SAUCE: a great blend of peppers, carrots, onion and lime juice; more flavour than most and not as vinegary.

OLD BAY SEASONING: mainly with seafood, but also enhances poultry.

PAPPY'S FAJITA SEASONING: a low-salt blend of spices and herbs; gives Pendery's a good run and is more readily available.

PAPPY'S LOUISIANA HOT SPICE: a blend of paprika, mustard, cumin, cayenne and fine herbs; the Louisiana taste you would find in New Orleans.

PAPPY'S SALT-FREE SEASONING: my favourite meat and poultry seasoning. By mail order.

PENDERY'S FAJITA SEASONING: the real taste of southwest cooking. By mail order.

PENDERY'S SICILIAN SPICE AND ITALIAN SPICE: two excellent blends of spices for flavouring and adding zip to pasta sauces. By mail order.

SONOMA MARINATED TOMATOES: naturally dried and packed in olive oil, these tomatoes from California are the most supple and tasty.

TELLICHERRY BLACK PEPPER: the ultimate black pepper; just taste the difference.

TIGER SAUCE: fairly hot but leaning to the sweet side.

WATKIN'S SALSA SPICE MIX: top-quality spices and herbs for a flavourful fresh tomato salsa.

WHITE PEPPER: to add heat without changing the flavour.

WHOLE MEXICAN OREGANO: not as overpowering as Mediterranean oregano.

Barbecue Beverages

Beer is far and away the favourite drink with barbecue foods. Darryl Frost, executive chef of a recently opened barbecue restaurant in Vancouver, recommends a light lager with seafood and chicken, an ale or bitter with beef brisket, and a stout with heavier-tasting pork dishes.

If you prefer wine, here are some general guidelines from Paul Warwick, who judges wines in British Columbia and California:

With salmon, Paul recommends a Chardonnay.
With a beef brisket, he suggests a Cabernet.
With ribs, a Merlot.
With grilled chicken, a Pinot Noir.
With spicy barbecued foods, a Gewürztraminer for those who prefer white wines and a Shiraz for the red-wine drinkers.

Spice Rubs for Meat

Competition barbecue chefs are always asked which is most important, the spices they rub on the meat, the wood they cook over or the sauce they baste with. Most place a high value on their spice rub and guard the secret of that mixture. I, on the other hand, doctor a purchased spice rub and am perfectly willing to share my recipe, which is below.

Spices and herbs for barbecue and grilling are either combined in a spice rub or sprinkled on the meat. The most commonly used are salts (table, sea, kosher, seasoned, celery, onion or garlic), regular white sugar (brown forms lumps because of its moisture content), Spanish or American paprika (for colour and mellowing of other spices), black pepper and a purchased chili powder (which is usually a blend of several powdered chilies, salt and cumin).

Other ingredients are added in smaller amounts to spice rubs or are sprinkled on grilled meats and vegetables: epazote (a pungent herb used extensively in TexMex grilling); dehydrated garlic and onion granules (rather than powder which forms lumps); Jamaican jerk (a hot sauce used as a rub); lemon powder (which is dried lemon zest); mustard flour (dry mustard powder); cayenne pepper; dried and crushed red peppers; salt-free seasoning; and tabil (a mix of coriander, caraway, garlic and chili powder).

In Cajun cooking, batches of spice rubs are mixed and ground to a fine powder, which is rubbed on meat, poultry or fish and cooked on hot cast-iron grills or frying pans. This produces the blackened effect and a pungent flavour. In the indirect method of barbecue, these spice rubs give a more subtle result because they are not seared by extreme heat.

If you wish to make your own rub, start with equal amounts of white sugar and salts (any combination of those mentioned above). Add dehydrated onion and garlic because onion and garlic powders tend to produce lumps. Choose from the spices and herbs I've already mentioned and from the following dried ingredients, which are best added as a minor note: allspice, basil, cayenne, celery seed, cinnamon, parsley, oregano, rosemary, savoury powder, thyme, mustard flour, lemon zest and lemon pepper.

Choosing spices and herbs for a rub is a matter of taste. Do not, however, let any one be overpowering and remember that the dry mixture will taste different on the cooked food. It takes time and practice to produce a good barbecue rub. I can recommend these tested recipes.

In each case, simply combine the ingredients, mix well and store in a cool dry place.

My competition barbecue rub

2 cups	Pappy's Salt-free Seasoning
1/4 cup	white sugar
1/2 cup	sea salt
1/4 cup	tellicherry black pepper

Basic barbecue rub

1 cup	sugar
1/2 cup	paprika
1/4 cup	chili powder
1/4 cup	seasoned salt
1/4 cup	celery salt
1/4 cup	onion salt
1/4 cup	garlic salt
1/4 cup	black pepper
1 tbsp	savoury powder
1 tbsp	Cajun spice
1/2 tbsp	coriander powder

Salt-free barbecue rub

1/2 cup	sugar
1/4 cup	salt-free seasoning
1/4 cup	chili powder
2 tbsp	black pepper
2 tbsp	garlic granules
2 tbsp	onion granules
1 tbsp	Mexican oregano powder

Creole barbecue rub

1 lb	kosher salt
1 cup	black pepper
1/4 cup	paprika
1/4 cup	dried and crushed red chilies
2 tbsp	garlic granules
1 tbsp	MSG

Barbecue sprinkle

4 tbsp	sea salt
3 tbsp	paprika
2 tbsp	chili powder
2 tbsp	black pepper
1 tbsp	garlic granules
1 tsp	cumin power
1/2 tsp	cayenne pepper

Salt-free lemon and herb barbecue rub

1 tbsp	parsley flakes
1 tbsp	lemon powder
2 tsp	garlic granules
2 tsp	basil
2 tsp	celery seed
1 tsp	onion granules
1/2 tsp	mustard flour
1/4 tsp	powdered rosemary

Wild game barbecue rub

2 tbsp	kosher salt
1 tbsp	paprika
1 tbsp	black pepper
1 tbsp	onion granules
1/2 tbsp	garlic salt
1 tsp	rosemary powder
1 tsp	Mexican oregano powder
1 tsp	basil powder
1/2 tsp	thyme powder
1/2 tsp	white pepper
1/2 tsp	cumin powder

Seafood barbecue rub

1 tbsp	paprika
1/2 tbsp	sea salt
2 tsp	black pepper
1 tsp	garlic powder
1 tsp	lemon powder
1/2 tsp	coriander
1/2 tsp	parsley flakes
1/4 tsp	cayenne pepper

Marinades

To prepare any of these marinades, whisk the ingredients together. Place the meat you want to marinate in a glass dish. Pour the marinade over top, cover with food wrap and marinate overnight. Turn the meat several times during this period. Cubed meat for kabobs should marinate only 4 to 6 hours.

Wine marinade

1 cup	dry red wine
½ cup	olive oil
¼ cup	parsley, minced
3	garlic cloves, minced
1 tsp	rosemary powder
½ tsp	ginger powder
½ tsp	black pepper

Lemon marinade

3 tbsp	fresh lemon juice
3 tbsp	olive oil
1 tbsp	brown sugar
½ tsp	Mexican oregano powder
½ tsp	black pepper
¼ tsp	garlic powder

Teriyaki marinade

½ cup	soy sauce
½ cup	grapefruit juice
¼ cup	olive oil
¼ cup	brown sugar
2 tbsp	oyster sauce
1 tbsp	garlic powder
1 tsp	ginger powder
1 tsp	Chinese five-spice powder
½ tsp	Tabasco

Use the same procedure as above but marinate for only 3 to 5 hours.

Chicken marinade

½ cup	white vinegar
¼ cup	fresh lime juice
¼ cup	olive oil
1 tbsp	Worcestershire sauce
1 tbsp	sea salt
1 tbsp	parsley, minced
4	garlic cloves, minced
1 tsp	Mexican oregano powder
1 tsp	black pepper

Use the same procedure as above but marinate chicken for only 2 to 4 hours.

Mop Sauces

These are thin sauces that some people like to apply in the early stages of barbecuing. I don't use a mop sauce, but Pat swears by hers and has won a competition using it.

Basic barbecue mop sauce

2 cups	beef stock
1/3 cup	olive oil
1	large onion, quartered
2 tbsp	mustard flour
2 tbsp	black pepper
3	large garlic cloves, minced
1	large bay leaf
2 tbsp	sea salt

Place all the ingredients in a stainless steel pot and bring to a boil. Reduce the heat and simmer for 30 minutes. Use a clean dish mop to apply to the meat during the cooking time.

Pat's barbecue mop sauce

1 quart	beef stock
1 cup	olive oil
1/2 cup	Worcestershire sauce
1/2 cup	cider vinegar
1	large onion, minced
4 oz	Tabasco
1 tbsp	salt
1 tbsp	mustard flour
1/2 tbsp	bay leaf powder

Place all the ingredients in a stainless steel pot and bring to a boil. Reduce the heat and simmer for 1 hour. Allow to stand overnight before using. Apply as above.

All-purpose barbecue mop sauce

1 cup	fresh lemon juice
1/2 cup	olive oil
1/4 cup	soy sauce
1 tsp	salt
1 tsp	black pepper
1/2 tsp	rosemary powder
1/2 tsp	marjoram powder

Combine all the ingredients in a stainless steel pot and simmer for 15 minutes. Apply as above.

Salt-free barbecue mop sauce

1 cup	beef stock
1/2 cup	olive oil
1/2 cup	cider vinegar
1/3 cup	fresh lemon juice
1/4 cup	shredded onion
1 tbsp	Mexican oregano powder
2 tbsp	salt-free seasoning

Place all the ingredients in a stainless steel pot and simmer for 30 minutes. Allow to cool overnight. Stir well and apply as above.

Barbecue Sauces

*Use these sauces in the final stages of barbecuing
or as dips for cooked meats.*

Basic barbecue sauce

3 cups	ketchup
1 cup	brown sugar
½ cup	vinegar
2 tbsp	chili powder
2 tbsp	garlic powder
1 tbsp	Worcestershire sauce
1 tbsp	black pepper
1 tbsp	salt
1 tbsp	savoury powder
½ tsp	ginger powder
½ tsp	cayenne pepper

Combine all the ingredients in a stainless steel pot, bring to
a boil and stir well. Lower the heat and simmer for approximately 30 minutes, blending and stirring often.

Oklahoma hot barbecue sauce

4 cups	chili sauce
1 cup	water
1 cup	molasses
½ cup	onion, minced
½ cup	cider vinegar
¼ cup	fresh lemon juice
3 tbsp	Worcestershire sauce
2 tbsp	soy sauce
3 tbsp	mustard flour
2	garlic cloves, minced
2 tbsp	Tabasco
½ tsp	cayenne pepper

Combine all the ingredients in a stainless steel pot, bring to
a boil and stir well. Lower the heat and simmer for 1 hour,
stirring often. If too thick, add a little water.

Plum barbecue sauce

14 oz	canned purple plums
6 oz	canned frozen lemonade
½ cup	green onions, minced
¼ cup	chili sauce
2 tsp	prepared mustard
2 tsp	ginger powder
2 tsp	soy sauce
2 tsp	liquid honey

Purée the plums in a food processor. Combine all the ingredients in a stainless steel pot, bring to a boil and stir well. Lower the heat and simmer for 1 hour, stirring often. If too thick, add a little water.

Houston barbecue sauce

¼ lb	butter
3	large garlic cloves, minced
1	onion, minced
1	large lemon, diced
4 cups	ketchup
¼ cup	Worcestershire sauce
¼ cup	brown sugar
¼ cup	vinegar
¼ cup	chili powder
16 oz	V8 juice
1 tbsp	black pepper

Melt the butter in a stainless steel pot, add the garlic, onion and lemon and sauté until limp. Add the remaining ingredients and simmer for 1½ hours, or until the sauce thickens, stirring often. If the sauce is too thick, add V8 juice.

Sweet hoisin barbecue sauce

⅓ cup	liquid honey
¼ cup	hoisin sauce
¼ cup	cider vinegar
¼ cup	soy sauce
2	large garlic cloves, minced
1 tsp	fresh ginger, grated

Place all the ingredients in a glass bowl. Mix and blend well.

GRILLED APPETIZERS

BRIE
with DRIED TOMATOES and GARLIC

A slight French twist on the barbecue. This makes an impressive appetizer or after-noon snack.

1	5-oz round of brie cheese
2 tbsp	dried tomatoes (packed in oil), minced fine
1	large garlic clove, minced
½ tbsp	fresh parsley, minced fine
¼ tsp	coriander powder
½	lime
	black pepper

Combine the dried tomatoes, garlic, parsley and coriander in a bowl. Blend well and allow to sit at room temperature for at least 20 minutes. Toss the mixture and then spread evenly over the top of the brie. Have your barbecue pre-heated at medium to high heat (350 to 400°F). Place the brie in the coolest area of the barbecue, not directly above the heat. Barbecue for approximately 10 minutes, or until the cheese just begins to melt.

Using a wide spatula, carefully place the brie on a serving dish. Squeeze the juice of the lime over it, sprinkle with black pepper and serve with melba toast or toasted baguette bread.

Serves 4

BARBECUE GARLIC
bulbs

1 large head of garlic
¼ tsp olive oil
    paprika

Slice off just enough of the top of the garlic head to expose the cloves. Place it on a piece of aluminum foil. Sprinkle the exposed cloves with paprika and then drizzle with the olive oil. Wrap tightly in the foil and place on the pre-heated barbecue on the unfired section of the grid over a medium to high heat (350 to 400°F) for 25 to 30 minutes. Cut open the foil to expose the garlic and allow it to cool. Squeeze the cloves onto toasted baguette bread slices and serve.

Always a cooking show favourite, this one will have your neighbours peeking over the fence. The aroma of garlic in the air always reminds me of the Gilroy Garlic Festival in California.

Barbecue Garlic Paste

A slight French twist on the barbecue. This makes an impressive appetizer or afternoon snack.

3 garlic heads, barbecued as above
1 tsp butter, soft
¼ tsp fresh cilantro, minced very fine
¼ tsp fresh lime juice

Squeeze all the cloves into a bowl and blend in the butter, cilantro and lime juice. Use as a spread on hamburgers, on bread or with barbecue meats.

green-shelled MUSSELS
with ARUGULA

These mussels are imported frozen from New Zealand. Cleaned and in the half shell, they are ready for use after defrosting. Fresh mussels are available at Asian stores year-round.

1 pkg	frozen green-shelled mussels in the half shell
⅓ cup	olive oil
¼ cup	arugula, minced
6	large garlic cloves, minced fine
1 tsp	hot sauce (e.g., Melinda's XXXtra Hot Sauce)

Defrost the frozen mussels in the refrigerator for 18 hours as directed on the package.

Combine the remaining ingredients in a bowl and set aside. Arrange the mussels on the preheated barbecue. Distribute the olive oil mixture equally into each shell, close the lid and barbecue the mussels over a high heat (400°F) for 10 to 15 minutes or until the meat plumps up and the oil sizzles around the edges of the shell.

Transfer the mussels to a serving dish and serve with sourdough bread.

Serves 4

RASPBERRY SALMON appetizer

1	2-lb spring salmon fillet
1/3 lb	fresh raspberries, or individually frozen
3	large Anaheim peppers
1 tbsp	fresh lime juice
3 tbsp	liquid honey
1/2 tsp	celery seed
1/2 tsp	savoury powder
1/4 cup	fresh parsley, minced
3 tbsp	sweet hot sauce (e.g., Tiger Sauce)
1 tbsp	butter
1/4 cup	fresh chives, minced fine
1 tsp	black pepper

A cooking show favourite. A great lead-in for a seafood main course, such as cod.

Remove the belly and pin bones from the fillet (using bone tweezers if you have a pair). Remove the seeds and veins from the peppers and mince the flesh. (I wear disposable latex gloves to protect my hands from the oil which can burn skin.)

To prepare a raspberry sauce, heat and toss the peppers, without adding oil, in a nonstick frying pan until limp. Add the lime juice, liquid honey, celery seed and savoury. Heat on low for an additional 3 minutes, but do not boil. Transfer this mixture to a nonstick saucepan. Stir in the parsley and sweet hot sauce. Cover with a lid and set aside.

With a sharp knife, score the salmon diagonally in both directions, cutting approximately half way to the skin and creating a diamond pattern on the surface. Place the salmon on the preheated barbecue, skin side down over a medium heat (350°F). Grill for 10 minutes.

While the salmon is cooking, melt the butter into the Anaheim pepper mixture and bring to a low heat. Coarsely chop the raspberries and gently stir them into this mixture. When heated, replace the lid and remove from the heat.

Using a basting brush, wipe off any white residue (fish oil) from the salmon. With a sharp knife open the slits you made in the fillet. Fill them with the chives and sprinkle with the black pepper, using all of it. Replace the lid, turn the heat to high (400°F) and cook the salmon for 8 to 10 minutes more.

Remove the fish from the barbecue by inserting spatulas between the skin and the flesh. Lift the fillet off but leave the skin on the grid.

Place the skinless salmon fillet on a serving platter. Heat the raspberry sauce and spoon into the slits and over the fillet.

Serves 6

jalapeño pepper
BOMBS

12 large jalapeño peppers
6 oz Monterey Jack cheese, grated fine
3 oz chorizo sausage, fried
   and minced fine
   olive oil

A culinary fusion of Mexican peppers, Portuguese sausage and California cheese. The response to this appetizer is usually, "Wow!"

Prepare a gas barbecue for the indirect method of cooking by igniting one or two of the burners on a medium to high heat (350 to 400°F).

Wearing latex gloves to protect your hands from the oil of the peppers, make a slit along the length of each pepper and remove the seeds with a small spoon. Rinse the peppers under cold water and dry well with paper towels.

Blend the cheese and sausage in a small bowl. Stuff each pepper with this mixture and close the slit with a toothpick pushed through each pepper crosswise at an angle.

Arrange the peppers, slit side up on the unfired side of the barbecue. Barbecue at medium to high heat until the cheese just begins to melt.

Using tongs, gently move the jalapeños directly over high heat (400°F). Grill the peppers until lightly charred, rolling them back and forth and brushing them lightly with the olive oil. Do not roll them over entirely because the cheese will ooze out.

Serves 4 to 6

amatory OYSTERS
on the HALF SHELL

An adaptation of my award-winning salmon recipe and just as delicious. An all-season appetizer.

Of the four main species of oyster, the Pacific has the deepest shell, making it perfect for barbecue or grilling.

24	small live oysters, in their shells, washed and scrubbed
1/4 cup	olive oil
6	garlic cloves, minced fine
4 tbsp	fresh parsley, minced fine
2 tbsp	dried tomatoes (packed in oil), minced fine
1 tsp	black pepper
1/4 tsp	salt
1 lb	fresh spinach, washed and torn into bite-size pieces

Combine the olive oil, garlic, parsley, dried tomatoes, black pepper and salt in a glass jar. Cover with a lid and shake well.

Shuck the oysters, leaving the meat in the deeper half of the shell. Arrange the oysters on the preheated barbecue. Spoon the garlic mixture equally into each half shell. Close the lid and grill over a medium to high heat (350 to 400°F) for 10 to 12 minutes, or until the oysters bubble around their edges.

As the oysters are grilling, wilt the spinach by heating without oil in a nonstick frying pan over a low heat for approximately 7 minutes. Divide the spinach equally on plates and arrange the oysters on the spinach.

Serves 4

AROMATIC
WING APPETIZERS

30	chicken wings, separated at the joint
	black pepper
	salt
2 tbsp	olive oil
2 tbsp	white pepper
2 tbsp	fresh ginger, grated
2 tbsp	fresh parsley, minced
4	large garlic cloves, minced very fine
1 tbsp	fresh basil, chopped
1/2 cup	fresh cilantro, minced fine
1 tbsp	brown sugar
1/4 cup	fresh lime juice
2 tbsp	balsamic vinegar

If you prepare the zesty dressing the day before, you will be able to serve this appetizer in 30 minutes on the following day.

Prepare the dressing by whisking the olive oil, white pepper, ginger, parsley, garlic, basil, cilantro and brown sugar in a glass bowl. Combine the lime juice and balsamic vinegar in a small jar. Cover with a lid, shake well and then slowly whisk into the oil and spices. Mix well to produce a runny, pastelike consistency.

Rub the chicken wings with black pepper and salt. Grill over a medium heat (350°F), turning the wings often until they are well browned and crispy.

Transfer the chicken wings to a large glass serving bowl. Drizzle the dressing over top, toss gently and serve.

Serves 4

EUROPEAN
FLAT BREAD

Every European country will have its own moniker for this recipe.

Add some minced onion, herbs or cheese to give it your own spin.

2 cups	white flour
½ pkt	quick-rise instant yeast
1 tbsp	olive oil
1 tbsp	fresh rosemary, minced
½ tsp	sea salt
1-1½ cups	warm water
	olive oil
	coarse sea salt

Combine the flour, yeast, olive oil, rosemary and salt in a bowl. Mix with just enough warm water to produce a pliable dough. Transfer the dough to a floured board and knead until it is smooth and elastic in texture.

Place in an oiled bowl. Cover with food wrap and allow to stand at room temperature for at least an hour until the dough has doubled in size.

Lightly knead the dough. Separate it into four balls. Flatten the balls and roll out into rounds approximately 4 inches in diameter and ¼ inch thick. Cover the flats with food wrap and again allow them to stand at room temperature until double in thickness.

Prepare a gas barbecue for the indirect method of cooking (page 42). Place the flats on the oiled, unfired section of the grid. Brush the bread with olive oil and sprinkle with the coarse sea salt. Close the lid and barbecue indirectly at medium heat for approximately 30 minutes or until the flats puff up and turn a golden brown in colour.

Yields 4

LOW
AND
SLOW

INDIRECT COOKING OVER
CHARCOAL OR GAS

LOW AND SLOW

I DIDN'T BELIEVE IT when I first heard you could cook tough cuts of beef on a barbecue. Pat and I were at a chili competition in Washington when someone mentioned a beef brisket barbecue in Woodinville, farther south in the state. Pat and I drove down to see. They were handing out slices of brisket half an inch thick. I expected it to be tough, but you could cut it with a fork.

This is what barbecue is about in the southern United States. Food is cooked at low temperatures for long hours. It's also known as the indirect method because food is not placed directly over hot coals or a lit burner.

Barbecue cookbooks may be filled with recipes for various cuts of meat, but the low and slow technique is the same in any part of the southern United States. The biggest difference is in the sauces, marinades or spice rubs.

The recipes in this chapter are all cooked at low temperatures for a long time, some over charcoal, some on gas and some on either type of barbecue.

Low and slow cooking requires more time than fast grilling, but not necessarily the constant presence of the cook. I put a beef brisket on and go out for two hours. When I get back, I turn it, tend to the fire and leave it again for another two or three hours. For a turkey, however, I hang around with my spray bottle to give it the occasional spritz of apple juice.

Cold weather may not affect low and slow cooking on a gas barbecue, but a charcoal fire may need more tending. If the day is cold *and* windy, I'd suggest you turn your oven on and barbecue tomorrow.

Indirect cooking over charcoal and wood

Before you begin to cook, check the amount of charcoal required (See the Low and Slow Cooking Chart, page 61). I light my charcoal in a chimney starter, because it takes less than ten minutes for the coals to reach the ashen-gray, ready-to-cook stage. I pile about three to four pounds of charcoal (or briquettes) into the chimney, which I place over two lit starter sticks on a fireproof surface outdoors. When the coals are hot, they can be poured into a barbecue kettle or lifted in with tongs. Coals can be set alight in the barbecue but they will take thirty minutes to reach cooking heat.

Kettle barbecues

To prepare a Weber kettle or similar charcoal barbecue for the indirect method of cooking, pile hot coals on one side of the kettle or pile three to four pounds of charcoal on one side and set alight. Rub the grate with a paper towel dipped in vegetable oil before you place it in the barbecue. Close the lid, leaving the vents in the lid and at the bottom of the kettle open. When the coals are ashen-gray, place a disposable aluminum bread loaf pan full of water on the grate over the coals. This will counteract the dry heat of a charcoal fire.

Put the food on the grate opposite the coals. Close the lid, allow the barbecue to heat to the temperature indicated in the recipe (usually 225°F) and adjust the vents in the base and the lid to maintain this temperature. If your barbecue does not have a temperature gauge, hang an instant-read thermometer on the lip of the kettle or place an oven-testing thermometer on the grid. Add wood chips or chunks as specified in each recipe.

From time to time, you will have to add more fuel. If you make hot coals in a chimney starter, you can pour them into the kettle without losing much cooking time. Adding cold charcoal to the hot coals in the kettle will slow down the cooking. In either case, remove the water pan, food and grid and add the fuel. Replace the grid, food and water pan. Close the lid with the vents open. Adjust the vents when the new charcoal is burning well or the recommended cooking temperature has again been reached.

INDIRECT COOKING OVER CHARCOAL OR GAS

Water smokers

A water smoker is about three feet tall and eighteen inches in circumference – like an elongated fire hydrant. It has a dome-shaped top lid, two cooking grids eight inches apart (food can be cooked on both grids), and a water pan which hooks in place under the bottom grid. A door on the side gives access to the water pan and the coals. Vents on the lid regulate the temperature.

When using a unit like this, first oil the grids. Then pre-heat three to four pounds of charcoal or briquettes in a chimney starter and transfer the coals to the smoker using tongs. Distribute the coals evenly in the bottom. Fill the water pan; I use a long-spouted watering can. When the temperature gauge reaches cooking heat, place the food on a grid, close the lid and adjust the vents to maintain the cooking temperature. The water will simmer throughout the cooking period. Add more water and coals every two to three hours.

Barbecue cookers

Large charcoal-burning units, such as my Pitt's and Spitt's, have a separate firebox on one end. Heat is drawn by convection into the cooking area and exits through a chimney. A damper on the firebox and a chimney vent allow the temperature to be regulated. The bottom of the cooking area under the grate is rounded and holds the water.

Preheat eight pounds of charcoal in a chimney starter (make two batches of four pounds each) and load the hot coals into the firebox. Add a couple of two-foot-long logs of apple wood. This is enough fuel for four to five hours. Oil the grid with oil-soaked paper towels. Put about an inch of water in the bottom of the cooking barrel, which will give enough moisture for ten hours of cooking. In about five minutes, when the cooking area has heated to the temperature indicated in the recipe, put whatever you are cooking on the grid, close the lid and adjust the damper and vents to maintain the correct temperature.

Indirect cooking on a gas barbecue

Slow cooking on a gas barbecue is straightforward. The heat in the barbecue is kept low by using only one or two burners, and food is placed on the grid over an unfired area.

My gas barbecue is a Weber with three burners – in the front, centre and rear. Lighting the front burner on medium and putting food in the rear produces excellent results.

If your barbecue has only two burners, you will turn only one burner on, but it will be harder to maintain a low temperature because these barbecues tend to heat hotter with one burner on than a three-burner barbecue does with two burners on. Watch the temperature and if it begins to rise, open the lid of the barbecue a crack.

Make sure you have enough propane. A full tank has more than enough fuel to cook a turkey. I always have a full spare tank on hand.

Wipe the grid with paper towels dipped in vegetable oil. Light one or two burners. They may be on one side or at the front or back.

With the lid closed, allow the unit to heat to the temperature indicated in the recipe. Place the food on an unfired section of the grid and close the lid.

It is not necessary to use a tray of water in a gas barbecue because the heat is not as dry. A smoky flavour can be obtained by placing a packet of herbed wood chips on the grid above the fired area.

texas
BEEF BRISKET

*A true Texan dish –
low and slow – using
charcoal, with wood
as an option. I bar-
becue about 300
briskets a year,
either at home, in
competition cooking
or for fund-raising
events. Cooked
slowly, they are
always fork-tender.
This recipe could
also be used for
prime rib roast,
baron of beef, chuck
roast or any cut of
beef weighing 6 to 10
pounds. The cooking
times on most char-
coal barbecues will
be approximately an
hour a pound for all
these cuts.*

1 6-lb beef brisket, not trimmed, and
    fat cap left intact
4 tbsp Basic Barbecue Rub (page 26)
¼ cup barbecue sauce (purchased or any on
    pages 29–30)

Prepare your charcoal barbecue for the indirect method of
cooking described in the introduction to this chapter. If
you choose to add wood to the barbecue, do so only during
the first 2 to 3 hours. Check the water pan for evaporation.

Sprinkle the entire brisket with the spice rub, using it
all. Place the beef on the grid, fat side down, and barbecue
at 225°F for 2 hours. Don't open the lid for a peek; just let it
be. After this time, replenish the coals and water, turn the
brisket over and barbecue it undisturbed for 2 to 3 hours
more at the same temperature. Baste it lightly with the barbecue sauce during the last half hour.

When the internal temperature reaches 175 to 180°F,
remove the brisket from the barbecue and allow to stand
for 15 minutes. Slice across the grain at ¼-inch intervals
and serve.

Serves 4 to 6

Oven barbecue beef brisket

You can barbecue beef brisket in the
oven and produce the same tender meat.
Preheat the oven to 225°F. Add ½ inch of
water to a shallow pan – a disposable,
rectangular aluminum roasting pan is
ideal. Sit two 10-inch square cake cooling
racks on the lip formed by the edge of the
pan. They will overlap in the middle.

Put the brisket, rubbed with the
spice mix, on the racks, fat side down,
and set the pan on an oven rack which is
4 or 5 inches from the bottom element.

As the beef cooks, the water will
keep it moist, and any fat will drip into
the water, keeping the oven clean. It's
unlikely that you will have to replenish
the water.

Roast and baste as directed in the
main recipe.

melt-in-your-mouth BARON OF BEEF

1	5-lb baron of beef (top round)
¼ cup	Salt-free Barbecue Rub (page 26)
4 tbsp	sea salt
	apple juice

Low and slow on a gas barbecue or over charcoal and wood. The two styles produce different tastes, but both are delicious.

Prepare a charcoal barbecue *or* a gas barbecue for the indirect method of cooking described in the introduction to this chapter. For a charcoal barbecue, add wood if you choose, but only during the first 2 to 3 hours. Check the water pan for evaporation.

Sprinkle the entire roast with the barbecue spice rub and the sea salt, using all of each. Place the meat on the grid, fat side down and barbecue for 3 hours at 250°F. Resist the temptation to peek at it.

After this time, turn the roast over and barbecue for 1 to 2 hours more. Spray with apple juice if the meat tends to brown too soon. When the roast is well done (an internal temperature of 170°F), remove it from the barbecue and allow to stand for 15 minutes.

Slice across the grain when serving.

Serves 6 to 8

SUCCULENT
prime ribs

Low and slow on a gas barbecue or over charcoal.

Beef ribs are larger than pork ribs; half a rack for each person is ample. Either method of slow cooking will produce meat that will fall off the bone.

2 racks	prime rib bones
4 tbsp	Salt-free Barbecue Rub (page 26)
2 tbsp	sea salt
1/4 cup	barbecue sauce (purchased or any on pages 29–30)

Prepare a charcoal barbecue *or* a gas barbecue for the indirect method of cooking described in the introduction to this chapter. For a charcoal barbecue, add wood if you choose, but only during the first hour. Check the water pan for evaporation.

To strip the membrane off the bone side of the ribs, slip a paring knife between the bone and the membrane to release it. Work your fingertips under the membrane, grasp it tightly and pull it off the entire length of the rack. This will allow the spices, smoke and heat to enter the meat. Sprinkle both sides of the ribs with all of the meat spice rub and sea salt. Allow the ribs to sit at room temperature for half an hour.

Arrange the ribs on the unfired section of the grid and barbecue for 2 to 3 hours at 225° F. Turn the ribs several times during this time. When you can pull the end bone off, the ribs are done. Then turn the burners to high or open the vents on a charcoal barbecue and cook the ribs until they are well browned.

Oven barbecue prime rib bones

After removing the membrane (as described in the main recipe), arrange the rib bones on overlapping cake cooling racks placed on top of a disposable aluminum roasting pan, which has 1/2 inch of water in it. Put in a preheated 225° F oven 4 or 5 inches from the bottom element and cook as directed.

Remove the ribs from the barbecue and paint them with the barbecue sauce. Wrap them tightly in food wrap and allow to stand for 10 minutes before serving.

Serves 4 to 6

A barbecue
TRIO of meats

¾ lb	beef steak (top round), one piece, 1 inch thick
1 lb	veal steak, one piece, 1 inch thick
1 ½ lb	lean pork steak, one piece, 1 inch thick
3 tbsp	black pepper
1 tsp	sea salt
½ cup	shiitake mushrooms, minced fine
½ cup	celery heart, including leaves, minced fine
½ cup	parsley, minced
½ cup	fine bread crumbs
	sea salt

Low and slow on a gas barbecue or over charcoal. When this rolled roast is served, each slice will reveal rings of beef, veal and pork interspaced with the light bread and mushroom stuffing.

Prepare a charcoal barbecue *or* a gas barbecue for the indirect method of cooking described in the introduction to this chapter. For a charcoal barbecue, add wood if you choose, but only during the first hour. Check the water pan for evaporation.

Using a meat mallet, flatten each cut of meat to twice its size. This is best done between two pieces of wax paper. You will then have 3 pieces of meat of different sizes, with pork being the largest, followed by the veal and finally the beef.

Prepare the stuffing by blending the pepper, salt, mushrooms, celery, parsley and bread crumbs in a bowl, making sure that they are thoroughly and evenly mixed. Sprinkle each piece of meat with a third of the stuffing and stack them in layer, with the pork on the bottom, then the veal and last the beef. Roll the meat tightly from one end and tie every 2 inches with butcher's twine.

Rub the entire roast with sea salt. Place it directly above the heat and sear it all over. Move the roast to the unfired area of the grid and barbecue for approximately 2 hours at 225 to 250°F. Turn the roast several times during the cooking period.

The outside of the roast will be crusted. Wrap the roast in food wrap and allow to stand for 10 minutes to soften the crust before slicing.

Serves 4 to 6

MEMPHIS
barbecue ribs

In Tennessee barbecue, ribs are cooked over charcoal and wood to get the authentic smoky taste, but you can omit the wood if you choose.

Once when I was barbecuing these ribs in a competition, I had four racks on a small water smoker. The guy beside me was doing a thousand racks at the same time. He submitted the best for judging and froze the rest for his catering business.

4 racks	baby back ribs
2 tbsp	prepared mustard
5 tbsp	beer
1 tbsp	black pepper
4 tbsp	Basic Barbecue Rub or Salt-free Barbecue Rub (page 26)
2 lbs	pork fat, sliced ⅛ inch thick
¼ cup	barbecue sauce (purchased or any on pages 29–30)

Prepare a charcoal barbecue for the indirect method of cooking described in the introduction to this chapter. If you choose to add wood to the barbecue, do so only during the first 2 hours. Check the water pan for evaporation.

To strip the membrane off the bone side of the ribs, slip a paring knife between the bone and the membrane to release it. Work your fingertips under the membrane, grasp it tightly and pull it off the entire length of the rack.

Combine the mustard, beer and black pepper in a bowl. Lightly paint both sides of the ribs with this mixture and sprinkle with the spice rub. Allow to stand at room temperature for half an hour.

Place the ribs on the unfired section of the grid, bone side down. Barbecue for 2½ to 3 hours at 225 to 250°F, or until they turn to a mahogany colour. At this point, remove the ribs from the barbecue.

Place a layer of pork fat on the grid and put a rack of ribs on top of it. Continue with layers of fat and ribs, finally topping off the last rack of ribs with the remaining fat. Barbecue for another hour.

Remove the ribs from the barbecue and discard the pork fat. Baste the ribs with the barbecue sauce, wrap them tightly in food wrap and allow to stand for 10 minutes before serving to heat the sauce.

Serves 4

southern barbecue
PORK SHOULDER

1	5-lb pork shoulder, blade bone intact
3 tbsp	Basic Barbecue Rub (page 26)
1/2 cup	cider vinegar
2	small white onions, minced very fine
1/4 cup	barbecue sauce (purchased or any on pages 29–30)

Prepare a charcoal barbecue for the indirect method of cooking described in the introduction to this chapter. If you choose to add wood to the barbecue, do so only during the first 3 hours. Check the water pan for evaporation.

Sprinkle the entire roast with the spice rub, using it all. Place the roast on the unfired section of the grid and barbecue at 225°F for 6 hours. Resist the temptation to take a peek at the roast to see how it's doing. Open the lid of a kettle barbecue only to replenish the coals and fill the water pan.

Transfer the shoulder to a large cutting board and allow it to stand for 10 minutes. Take hold of the blade bone and pull it. It should come out easily with no meat on the bone. This is the test for a perfect barbecue pork shoulder.

Remove the crackling and set it aside. "Pull" and chop the meat and put it in a large bowl or pan. Gently stir in the vinegar, onions and barbecue sauce.

Place the meat on a large serving platter. Mince half the crackling as a garnish for the top of the meat.

Serve as a main course with grilled vegetables and Memphis Creamy Coleslaw.

Serves 4 to 6

When I cooked this recipe in Friday Harbor, Washington, a few years ago in a competition to qualify for Memphis in May (the famous Tennessee barbecue cookoff), I took first place.

Memphis-style barbecue pork shoulder can't be sliced; it is "pulled" – pulled apart with a fork. I like to serve it with grilled vegetables and Memphis Creamy Coleslaw.

Memphis creamy coleslaw

Make this a few hours ahead of time.

½ head	green cabbage, sliced and chopped very fine, by hand
1	large carrot, grated
1	small onion, minced fine
2 tsp	vinegar
1 tsp	black pepper
¼ tsp	salt
⅔ cup	mayonnaise
2 tbsp	sugar
1½ tsp	mustard powder
1 tsp	Melinda's XXXtra Hot Sauce

Place the cabbage, carrot and onion in a large glass bowl. Add the vinegar, black pepper and salt. Toss and refrigerate for 1 hour. Toss the coleslaw several times during this period.

Combine the mayonnaise, sugar, mustard and hot sauce in a bowl. If the mixture is too thick, add a little cream. Ladle over the cabbage and toss well. Refrigerate the coleslaw until you are ready to serve it.

Serves 4 to 6

louisiana BARBECUE pork

1	4-lb pork butt, boneless, rolled and tied
½ cup	garlic, minced
½ cup	onion, minced very fine
4 tbsp	sweet hot sauce (e.g., Tiger Sauce)
3 tbsp	prepared mustard
1 tbsp	Worcestershire sauce
1 tbsp	sea salt
1 tbsp	black pepper

Prepare a charcoal barbecue *or* a gas barbecue for the indirect method of cooking described in the introduction to this chapter. For a charcoal barbecue, add wood if you choose, but only during the first 1 to 2 hours. Check the water pan for evaporation.

Pierce the roast with a sharp knife, making 15 slits about an inch deep over the entire surface.

Combine the remaining ingredients in a bowl. Rub this mixture into all the slits and over the entire roast.

Place the roast on the unfired section of the grid and barbecue for 3 to 5 hours at 225°F. There is no need to turn the roast. Open the lid of the barbecue only to replenish the coals and water, if you are cooking over charcoal in a kettle barbecue.

Serves 6 to 8

Tennesseeans like their barbecue pork pulled and served with a tart accompaniment, but in Louisiana-style barbecue, a pork butt is rolled and tied so that it can be sliced. People in Louisiana prefer mustard and hot sauce with their pork. This recipe is done on a charcoal barbecue, with wood as an optional addition.

Oven barbecue Louisiana pork

Louisiana pork can be barbecued in the oven. Follow the method given for Oven Barbecue Beef Brisket (page 46). Prepare the pork butt as described above and cook it in the oven at 225°F until it reaches an internal temperature of 180°F.

barbecue ham WITH orange MARMALADE sauce

Every city has a butcher who cures his own hams. It's worth the effort to seek one out in order to get the best result for your efforts in this recipe. I barbecue this ham at Christmas and it looks and tastes fantastic. You can cook it on a charcoal or gas barbecue.

1	12-lb ham
	black pepper
1/4 cup	orange marmalade
1/8 cup	prepared mustard
1/3 cup	brown sugar
2 cups	apple juice

Prepare a charcoal barbecue *or* a gas barbecue for the indirect method of cooking described in the introduction to this chapter.

Do not add wood to the charcoal barbecue, but do check the water pan for evaporation.

It's easier to remove the rind after the ham has cooked for an hour. To begin cooking, score the rind and fat in a diamond pattern using a sharp knife. Sprinkle the surface liberally with black pepper, making sure that some falls into the cuts in the rind.

Put the ham on the unfired section of the grid and barbecue for an hour at 225°F. At this point, you should be able to pull the rind off, using your fingers or tongs. You may need a knife to cut any stubborn bits free.

Return the ham to the grid and barbecue for another hour. Now, using a pastry brush, paint the top and sides of the ham with the orange marmalade and then with the mustard. Finally pat on the brown sugar. Barbecue for another 2 hours. Don't turn the ham but spray it with apple juice during this final cooking period.

Serve with a spicy-but-sweet purchased barbecue sauce or with Houston Barbecue Sauce (page 30).

Serves 8

THE ULTIMATE
barbecue turkey

1	12-lb turkey
2 cups	lemon concentrate (Realemon)
1 tsp	black pepper
1 tsp	garlic salt
	paprika
	apple juice

Wash the turkey under cold water and drain well. Wash again, inside and out, with the lemon concentrate. Sprinkle the skin with black pepper, garlic salt and liberally with paprika. Allow to air dry for one hour.

Prepare a charcoal barbecue for the indirect method of cooking described in the introduction to this chapter. If you choose to add wood to the barbecue, do so only during the first 4 hours. Check the water pan for evaporation.

Place the turkey, breast up, on the grid and barbecue for 8 to 10 hours at 250°F until the internal temperature reaches 180 to 190°F. In the first 5 to 6 hours, open the lid only to replenish coals and water if you are using a kettle barbecue. Spray with the apple juice during the last 2 to 3 hours of cooking. This will keep the paprika moist and stop the skin from splitting.

Serves 6 to 8

The meat of barbecue turkey and whole chicken has a pink tinge. I always have to assure people that it's not undercooked.

This recipe is best on a charcoal barbecue. You will need about 25 pounds of briquettes.

citrus CHRISTMAS
TURKEY

Whenever I do a turkey, even in the oven, I soak it in a bath of sea salt, a method I learned from an American chef I met at a barbecue event. The flavour of the meat is enhanced by the salt soak. The fruit stuffing in this recipe sweetens the meat and makes a fine side dish.

This is best cooked on a gas barbecue.

1	12-lb turkey
	sea salt
2	pink grapefruits
1	small orange
	lemon concentrate (Realemon)
2 tbsp	fresh parsley, minced
1 tbsp	fresh cilantro, chopped
1 tsp	black pepper

Place the turkey in a large plastic bucket. Add 1 cup of sea salt and fill the bucket with cold water, covering the bird. Store in the refrigerator overnight.

Cut the grapefruits into eighths; remove the rind and pits. Trim off any white membrane and cut into 1-inch cubes. Put the cubes in a glass bowl. Mince the orange, along with its rind, add to the grapefruit and refrigerate overnight.

Prepare a gas barbecue for the indirect method of cooking described in the introduction to this chapter.

Pat the turkey dry with paper towels. Stuff with the fruit mixture, sprinkle with sea salt and place breast up on the unfired area of the barbecue. Barbecue for 5 to 7 hours at 250°F until the internal temperature of the turkey reaches 180°F. Spray with the lemon concentrate several times during the cooking period. This will stop the bird from becoming too dark.

Transfer the turkey to a cutting board to rest before carving. Remove the fruit from the cavity and place in a small saucepan. Add the parsley, cilantro and black pepper and stir well. Bring the fruit mixture to a boil, transfer to a glass bowl and serve with the turkey.

Serves 6 to 8

This chicken's a
HAM

1 3-lb chicken, deboned*
1 2-lb ham, boneless
4 large eggs, hard-boiled
1 tsp sea salt
1 tsp black pepper
apple juice

Core the ham, making a lengthwise tunnel the diameter of an egg. (Save the core for a morning omelette.)

Cut enough of the white off the ends of the eggs to expose the yolk. Slip the eggs in a line into the tunnel you made in the ham.

Stuff the ham lengthwise into the cavity of the chicken and sprinkle the bird with the sea salt and black pepper.

Prepare a charcoal barbecue *or* a gas barbecue for the indirect method of cooking described in the introduction to this chapter. Do not add wood to the charcoal barbecue, but do check the water pan for evaporation.

Place the chicken on the unfired section of the grid and barbecue for approximately 3 hours at 225°F. Spray with apple juice several times during the final hour of barbecuing to stop the bird from getting too dark in colour.

When the temperature tested in the thigh is 180°F, remove the thighs, legs and wings. Slice the bird crosswise at half-inch intervals. The oval slices will reveal the white of the chicken, the red of the ham, the snow-white of the egg and finally the yellow of the yolk.

Serves 4

What seems like a complex preparation can be made easier by having your butcher debone the chicken. The colourful rings of chicken, ham and egg make an impressive presentation that will wow guests.

Barbecue this over charcoal or gas.

*Deboning a chicken

With a sharp filleting knife, disjoint (but do not cut off) the thighs and wings, leaving as much skin uncut as possible. Slip your fingers into the cavity between the meat and the skeleton. Little by little, advance forward and around the entire skeleton, until all the meat is freed. You will be able to remove the bones easily. After the bird is stuffed, skewer the thighs, legs and wings into their original positions.

halved
CHICKENS

Done over charcoal (and wood if you wish), this is the most popular way to prepare barbecue chicken. The cooking time isn't overly long – about 2½ hours.

2	small chickens, halved
1 tbsp	black pepper
½ tsp	sea salt
½ cup	butter
¼ cup	fresh lime juice
1 tsp	paprika
½ tsp	celery salt
½ tsp	garlic powder
3 tbsp	barbecue sauce (purchased or any on pages 29–30)
3 tbsp	apple juice
2 tbsp	brown sugar

Prepare a charcoal barbecue for the indirect method of cooking described in the introduction to this chapter. If you choose to add wood to the barbecue, do so only during the first hour. Check the water pan for evaporation.

Place the chicken halves on a platter. Sprinkle both sides with black pepper and salt. Cover with food wrap and refrigerate for 1 hour.

Melt the butter in a saucepan. Stir in the lime juice, paprika, celery salt and garlic powder. Bring the mixture to a low simmer, remove from the heat and set aside.

Place the chicken halves on the grid, skin side up. Barbecue for approximately 2½ hours at 225° F. Brush often with the butter mixture.

Combine the barbecue sauce, apple juice and brown sugar in a small glass bowl. Baste the chicken twice with this mixture during the final 20 minutes of cooking, producing a nice glaze.

Arrange the chicken halves on a large serving platter and cover with food wrap. Allow to stand for 10 minutes before serving.

Serves 4

garlic leg of
LAMB

1	5-lb leg of lamb, trimmed of fat
6	large garlic cloves, sliced lengthwise
1 cup	cider vinegar
2 tbsp	balsamic vinegar
3 tbsp	grainy Dijon mustard
1 tbsp	black pepper
1 tbsp	rosemary powder

You can do this recipe over charcoal or gas. I've given a European touch to the lamb by adding garlic, which is not used much in southern American barbecue. I don't add wood to my charcoal when I'm cooking lamb. Even though I've tasted lamb smoked by the best chefs, I don't enjoy it.

Make 25 to 30 deep slits in the lamb and insert a slice of garlic into each one. Place the leg in a glass dish. Mix the vinegars together and pour over the lamb. Cover with food wrap and refrigerate for 12 to 24 hours. Turn the leg several times during the marinating period.

Prepare a charcoal barbecue *or* a gas barbecue for the indirect method of cooking described in the introduction to this chapter. Do not add wood to the charcoal barbecue, but do check the water pan for evaporation.

Remove the lamb from the marinade, pat dry with paper towels and set aside to reach room temperature.

Prepare a spread by blending the mustard, pepper and rosemary in a small bowl.

Place the lamb on the preheated barbecue directly over a medium to high heat (350 to 400°F) and sear the meat all over until it is well browned. Transfer to a cutting board and paint the entire leg with the mustard spread.

Reposition the lamb on the unfired area of the grid and barbecue at 250 to 300°F for 2½ to 3 hours until the internal temperature reaches 140°F. Transfer to a cutting board. Allow to stand for 10 minutes, slice thinly and serve.

Serves 4 to 6

CRUSTED
leg of LAMB

This is a different method, combining a preliminary grilling over high heat with low and slow indirect cooking on a gas barbecue. A confession: I used to butterfly the leg of lamb myself, but it's a lot of work. I now have my butcher do it.

1	5-lb leg of lamb, bone removed and butterflied
10	large garlic cloves, sliced into slivers
2 tbsp	coarse sea salt
1/4 cup	fine bread crumbs
1 tbsp	black pepper
1 tbsp	thyme powder
1/4 tbsp	fresh mint, minced very fine
	olive oil
1/4 cup	onion, minced fine

Make slits over the entire leg of lamb, rub the leg with the sea salt and stuff a garlic sliver into each slit.

Combine the bread crumbs, black pepper, thyme and mint in a glass bowl. Add just enough olive oil to make a paste. Blend the onions into the mixture and set aside.

Grill the lamb over high heat (400°F) until well charred on all sides and then remove to a cutting board.

If the bread-crumb mixture has thickened, add a little more olive oil to loosen the paste. Pat firmly on the butterflied – or cut – side of the lamb.

Adjust the burners for the indirect method of cooking: shut off one of the burners and have the other one or two on low to medium (250 to 350°F).

Return the leg of lamb to the unfired area of the barbecue with the bread-crumb mixture facing up. Barbecue for 2 1/2 to 3 hours until the topping is well crusted and the lamb reaches an internal temperature of 135 to 140°F.

Arrange on a serving platter and allow to stand for 10 minutes before slicing.

Serves 4 to 6

Barbecue Low and Slow Cooking Chart

Type	Weight	Charcoal (lbs)	Water (qts)	Wood chunks	Time (hrs)*	Test for doneness
Beef brisket	3–4 lbs	8–10	4	8–10	4–6	170°F internally
Baron of beef	3–5 lbs	8–10	4	6–8	3–4	170°F internally
Beef chuck roast	3–5 lbs	10	6	8–10	4–5	170°F internally
Beef short ribs	4 bones	10–15	6	6–8	5–6	Meat pulls away from bone
Prime rib bones	2 racks	10	6	4–6	4–5	Meat pulls away from bone
Pork butt (bone in)	4–6 lbs	10–15	8	8–10	5–7	Blade bone will pull out
Pork butt (rolled & tied)	3–5 lbs	8–10	6	6–8	4–5	170°F internally
Pork loin (boneless)	2–3 lbs	6–8	4	4–6	3–5	170°F internally
Pork side ribs	4 racks	8–10	6	4–6	3–4	Meat pulls away from bone
Pork baby back ribs	4 racks	6–8	4–6	2–3	2–3	Meat pulls away from bone
Ham (cured & smoked)	4–6 lbs	8–10	8	4–6	3	140°F internally
Ham leg (fresh)	8 lbs	15–20	8	10	6–8	180°F internally
Chicken (whole)	2–3 lbs	6–8	6	5	2–3	180°F internally
Chicken (halves)	4	6–8	6	4	2	Legs move easily
Turkey (whole)	10 lbs	25	10	10	9–10	180°F internally
Leg of lamb	4–6 lbs	10–15	6	6	4–5	160°F internally
Rack of lamb	3–4 lbs	6–8	5	4–6	2–4	Meat pulls away from bone

* Approximate cooking times at 225°F

My ALL-TIME FAVOURITE seafood dish is grilled scallops in their shells. During my ten years of commercial fishing when we picked up scallops in our nets, we'd bake them in a very hot oven until the shells opened. Then we'd add some olive oil and spices, and we'd eat the whole thing – the meat and the small adductor muscle, which is what we are usually served in restaurants. My recipe for Scallops on the Grill is a re-creation of those fit-for-a-king fishing boat feasts.

In grilling seafood on the barbecue, two common problems can be overcome by purchasing the right equipment. Some fish fillets, such as sole, rock cod and trout, are too delicate to be turned over on the grid. Placing the fish in a hinged, long-handled basket solves this problem.

GRILLED SEAFOOD

Some shellfish have the annoying habit of slipping through the grid into the fire. Solve that by buying a Teflon-coated, perforated grid sheet or basket.

Cooking time on the barbecue will be affected by the type of fire (whether it is gas, wood or charcoal) and the distance of the fish from the heat. Generally, however, most fish will cook on the barbecue in eight to ten minutes for each inch of thickness.

Sole and trout will take less time – about six minutes per inch.

Sea bass, tuna and snapper might need twelve to fourteen minutes per inch.

Shellfish should be cooked quickly. You can see when they are done: oysters and clams get plump and their edges begin to curl; scallops turn from clear/opaque to white/opaque; shrimp and prawns turn pink and become firm. Oysters, clams and mussels in the shell are done when the shell opens and the meat is plump.

Allow thirty minutes to grill lobster tails. (To prevent them from curling up, remove the belly skin with cooking

The Only Barbecue Salmon, p. 66

shears. Be sure to baste well while they are cooking.)

It will take twenty to thirty minutes to grill fresh crab. (Remove the body shell, clean out the innards, and crack the legs before cooking.)

I don't agree with the common advice to cook fish until it flakes easily; by then it's overcooked. Check the fish before the end of the estimated cooking time. With experience, you will notice a change in colour or translucency which indicates the fish is cooked.

You can add wood chips to a charcoal barbecue or place a package of wood chips in a gas barbecue to give a nice smoke flavour to your fish.

But don't barbecue fish in aluminum foil, unless you want it steamed.

Buy the freshest fish you can find at the market. Fresh fish will not have a fishy or ammonia odour. Whole fish will have slightly bulging, bright, clear, almost alive-looking eyes. The skin will be moist with shiny, tightly-adhered scales, and the gills will be close to the colour of blood. When gently pressed, the body will give slightly and then spring back into shape.

Fillets or steaks should be shiny. As fish is kept on ice, the flesh tends to lose its appealing shine. Do not buy any fish that appears discoloured, dry or slightly mushy.

Although previously frozen fillets will have lost the shine, they should retain their good taste and aroma if they have been frozen properly and not for a long time. If the fish is still frozen, don't buy it if you see discolouration, freezer burn, ice crystals or a hole in the package.

When touched, a lively live crab or lobster will go into an attack stance.

Mint and Citrus Tuna Steaks with Avocado and Orange Saltsa, p. 80

Very Good

THE ONLY
barbecue salmon

This is one of my easiest salmon recipes, which I adapted from one my mother used to prepare. In 1989 I took first place at the Washington State Fair using this recipe. Since then, it has always brought home a blue ribbon.

1	3-lb fresh salmon fillet, deboned
6	large garlic cloves, minced fine
1 tsp	salt
4 tbsp	fresh parsley, minced fine
2 tbsp	dried tomatoes (packed in oil), minced fine
¼ cup	olive oil

Remove the belly and pin bones from the fillet, using bone tweezers if you have a pair.

Crush and mince the garlic cloves. Sprinkle with the salt. Using a wide-bladed knife, grind the garlic into a pulp. Combine the garlic, parsley, dried tomatoes and olive oil in a jar. Cover with a lid and shake well to blend all the ingredients. Refrigerate until ready for use.

With a sharp knife, cut two lengthwise slits in the salmon fillet, dividing the surface of the fish into thirds. Cut to the skin, but not through it.

Spread half the garlic mixture over the fillet and into the slits. Place the fish on a preheated barbecue over a medium heat (350°F). Close the lid and grill for 15 minutes.

Spread the remaining garlic mixture on the fillet. Close the lid, turn the temperature to high (400°F) and grill 10 more minutes.

Remove the fish from the barbecue by inserting spatulas between the skin and the flesh, so that you can lift the fillet but leave the skin on the grid. I like to serve the skinless and boneless fillet on a bed of fresh spinach.

Serves 4 to 6

Very Good

SMOULDERING herbed SALMON with BUTTER and YOGURT basting sauce

2	1-lb fresh salmon fillets
	salt
½ cup	butter
¾ cup	yogurt
3 tbsp	fresh lime juice
1 tsp	coriander powder
1 tsp	black pepper
1	large bunch each, fresh dill, fennel and basil

If you like the three herbs involved, you will enjoy this style of barbecue. The steaming effect of the herbs penetrates deep into the salmon.

Remove the belly and pin bones from the salmon, using bone tweezers if you have a pair. Cover the fresh herbs with water and allow to soak until needed (a minimum of 10 minutes will do).

To prepare a basting sauce, melt the butter in a saucepan. Remove the saucepan from the heat and blend in the yogurt, lime juice, coriander and pepper.

Put the salmon in an oiled, long-handled fish basket and sprinkle with salt. Use some of the basting sauce to coat the fillet and put it on a preheated barbecue, skin side up, over a low to medium heat (250 to 350°F).

Barbecue until the flesh is lightly browned, approximately 6 to 8 minutes. Turn the salmon over, raise the heat to high (400°F) and cook for 5 minutes more. Remove from the barbecue and set aside. At this point the salmon will be three-quarters cooked.

Shake most of the water off the herbs and arrange them on the barbecue in a thick leafy bed (over the fire). With the heat high, place the fish skin side up on the herbs and cook with the lid closed for 5 to 8 minutes. The herbs will smoulder and flavour the fish.

Turn the fish over and baste with the remaining sauce. Close the lid and allow the herbs to smoulder for 5 minutes more. Do not open the lid during this time.

Serves 4 to 6

RISQUÉ
barbecue oysters

Oyster lovers usually eat their oysters plain, with a minimum of sauce. But I wanted to do something different, and so I played around with ideas until I came up with this saucy combination of ingredients. Eat these oysters with a baked potato and sautéed spinach.

2 doz	small oysters, in their shells, washed and scrubbed
2 tbsp	olive oil
½ cup	shallots, minced
2	large garlic cloves, minced fine
1 cup	V8 juice
½ cup	liquid honey
4 tbsp	grainy mustard
3 tbsp	fresh lime juice
2 tbsp	hot sauce (e.g., Melinda's XXXtra Hot Sauce)
1 tbsp	sweet hot sauce (e.g., Tiger Sauce)
1 tsp	salt

To prepare the sauce, heat the olive oil in a small saucepan. Sauté the shallots in the oil for approximately 8 minutes. Add the garlic and sauté for 5 minutes more. Stir frequently to keep the garlic from burning. Add the remaining ingredients and simmer for 10 minutes.

Place the oysters on a preheated barbecue, with the deep side of the shell on the bottom, and grill over a high heat (400°F) until the shells open.

While you hold the bottom shells with tongs, remove the top shells. Spoon some sauce over each oyster and cook for an additional 5 minutes.

Heat any remaining sauce, place in a bowl and serve with the oysters and baguette bread.

Serves 4

SCALLOPS
on the grill

8	large bay scallops
4 tbsp	olive oil
2	large garlic cloves, minced very fine
1/4 cup	fresh parsley, minced
1/2 tsp	black pepper
1/4 tsp	salt

Preheat your barbecue to 450°F.

Combine the last five ingredients in a small bowl. Place the scallops on the grid and barbecue at this temperature until the shells open. When they have opened, add equal amounts of the olive oil mixture to each scallop. Raise the heat to the highest level and cook for 2 to 3 minutes more.

Arrange the scallops on separate appetizer or dinner plates and serve with a bounty of baguette bread.

Serves 4

In restaurants we are served only the muscle that opens and closes the shell of the scallop, but there is enough meat and muscle in just two scallops for a good appetizer portion, while three or four would make a meal.

If you can't find bay scallops, you can substitute sea scallops.

(in their entirety)

FLAMING
ROCK COD

I first cooked this recipe on CBC Radio for the Vicky Gabereau Show. I have tried many variations on it, but this is the one that brings out the succulent flavour of this ocean-bottom fish. You may think a whole rock cod is ugly, but beauty is in the eye of the beholder. The presentation is sure to impress your guests.

1	3-lb fresh whole rock cod, cleaned, scaled and the head on
½ tbsp	thyme powder
½ tbsp	bay leaf powder
½ tbsp	black pepper
½ tbsp	salt
2 tbsp	brandy
4	large limes, cut into wedges
	olive oil

Make several diagonal cuts through the skin of the rock cod. To make it easier to serve the cooked fish, prepare it in this way: on the inside of the belly, cut through the rib bones on each side of the backbone, making sure not to cut into the meat. When the fish is cooked, you will be able to remove the bones easily and to open the fish flat.

Combine the thyme, bay leaf powder, black pepper and salt in a bowl. Rub half of this mixture on the inside of the cod. Rub the outside of the cod with some olive oil and the remaining spices.

Place the cod in a long-handled fish basket and grill over a high heat (400°F). Turn and baste with the olive oil often. This will take 20 to 30 minutes.

Remove and open the rock cod. Place it on its belly on a heated fireproof serving platter. Surround the fish with the lime wedges and pour warmed brandy over top. Carefully light the brandy and serve the flaming rock cod.

Serves 4

SNAPPER
kabobs with an orange-maple glaze

2   1-lb fresh red snapper fillets, boneless and skinless
½ tbsp   orange zest, fresh grated
½ tsp   mustard powder
¼ tsp   cumin powder
¼ tsp   salt
1 tbsp   undiluted frozen orange juice
1 tbsp   balsamic vinegar
⅓ cup   maple syrup

Snapper is a year-round favourite and probably one of the most versatile species that we harvest from the sea. The fresh flavour of orange will always complement a white fish such as this.

Cut the fillets in half, lengthwise and crosswise. This will give you 8 strips that are approximately 2 inches wide by 6 inches long. Thread the snapper strips on 8 skewers. To prevent the fillets from spinning, use two parallel skewers about half an inch apart. Place the kabobs on a cookie sheet and refrigerate.

Prepare a glaze by combining the orange zest, mustard powder, cumin and salt in a small saucepan. Stir in the orange juice and vinegar, making a light paste. Turn the heat on low and slowly drizzle in the maple syrup. Bring this to a simmer and cook for 3 to 5 minutes or until it thickens. Lower the heat and keep the sauce warm.

Have your barbecue preheated to a medium to high heat (350 to 400°F). Brush the grid with oil to prevent the kabobs from sticking.

Grill the strips for approximately 5 minutes. Turn the skewers twice during this time. Now, baste the kabobs lightly with the warm glaze, and grill for an additional 3 minutes. Turn the skewers only once.

Serves 4

RED HOT SNA

My relatives in California have taken me to a café in San Pedro where the Croatian owner serves snapper prepared like this. It's a little on the spicy side, but that doesn't interfere with the subtle flavour of the fish. Have rice as a side dish to moderate the spice.

2	¾-lb red snapper fillets, boneless with the skin on
¾ cup	olive oil
2 tbsp	raspberry vinegar
2 tbsp	cold water
4	large garlic cloves, minced fine
3 tbsp	hot sauce (e.g., Melinda's XXXtra Hot Sauce)
1 tbsp	cumin powder
1 tbsp	salt
	black pepper
2	Belgium endives, washed and coarsely chopped
1 head	butter lettuce, washed and coarsely chopped
2	large red bell peppers, julienned
2	large yellow bell peppers, julienned
6	large limes, cut into wedges
6	medium avocados, peeled and cut into wedges
	fresh tomato salsa (purchased or homemade)

To prepare a marinade, combine the olive oil, vinegar, cold water, garlic, hot sauce, cumin and salt in a glass jar. Cover with a lid, shake well and pour into a shallow glass dish.

Put the fillets in the marinade, skin side up, and refrigerate for 30 to 45 minutes. During this time move the fillets around a few times to stir up the marinade.

Put the bell peppers on a barbecue tray that prevents smaller items from falling through and grill them until they begin to char. Then move them to the coolest area of the barbecue.

PPER FILLETS

Grill the fillets, skin side up, over a medium to high heat (350 to 400°F) for 5 minutes. Carefully turn the fillets so the skin side is down. Sprinkle liberally with black pepper and grill for an additional 5 minutes, or until the flesh turns white and opaque. Baste the fillets often with the marinade during this cooking period.

Arrange the endive and butter lettuce on a large serving platter. Distribute the grilled bell peppers over top. Alternate lime and avocado wedges around the outer edge so they will surround the snapper when it is placed on the platter.

Remove the fish from the barbecue by inserting spatulas between the skin and the flesh. Lift the flesh off but leave the skin behind. Place the fillets on top of the vegetables. Serve with a fresh tomato salsa.

Serves 4 to 6

BARBECUE MONKFISH

with tomato and orange salsa

When I first purchased these fillets, I told my fishmonger that in their raw state they were fairly unattractive. He said, "No, they are downright ugly." Nevertheless, when cooked they turn a beautiful white colour. Because of its flavour and texture, monkfish is known in many parts of the world as lobster fish. Prepare the salsa earlier in the day to let the flavours blend.

4 6-oz monkfish fillets
½ cup butter, melted
½ tsp fresh lime juice
1 cup Fresh Tomato and Orange Salsa

Combine the melted butter and lime juice in a shallow glass baking dish. Add the fillets and allow to stand for 15 minutes at room temperature. Turn the fillets several times during this period.

Place the fillets on a preheated barbecue over a medium heat (350°F) for 12 to 15 minutes or until the fillets just begin to flake when checked with a fork. Turn and baste with the butter mixture several times during the cooking period.

Arrange the fillets on dinner plates, spoon equal amounts of Fresh Tomato and Orange Salsa on top and serve.

Serves 4

Fresh tomato and orange salsa

10 large plum tomatoes, peeled, seeded and ¼-inch diced
¼ cup green onion, white ends only, ⅛-inch diced
1 large orange
2 tbsp fresh cilantro, minced
1½ tbsp fresh lime juice
½ tsp dried and crushed red chilies
¼ tsp dried whole Mexican oregano
⅛ tsp garlic granules
⅛ tsp salt
⅛ tsp cumin powder

Peel the orange, removing as much of the white membrane as possible and separating it into its sections. Then gently dice the sections into ½-inch pieces.

Combine all the ingredients in a glass bowl, toss and refrigerate for 4 to 6 hours. Gently stir the salsa several times during this period. Allow to reach room temperature before serving.

Yields 3 cups (approximately)

SATAN'S
SEA BASS

4	8-oz pieces sea bass
¾ cup	olive oil
10	large garlic cloves, minced fine
½ cup	roasted red bell peppers, coarsely chopped
¼ cup	fresh parsley, minced
3 tbsp	Conimex Sambal Oelek
1 tbsp	coriander powder
½ cup	sunflower seeds, toasted

Place the sea bass in a glass dish in a single layer.

Prepare a marinade by combining the oil, garlic, peppers, parsley, Sambal Oelek and coriander in a bowl. Pour half of the mixture over the sea bass and refrigerate for 30 to 45 minutes. Place the remainder of the marinade in a saucepan and keep warm.

Grill the bass on a preheated barbecue over a medium to high heat (350 to 400°F) for 4 to 6 minutes a side, turning only once. Baste each side liberally with the marinade while cooking. Remove and arrange on a serving platter.

Heat the reserved marinade just to the boiling point. Immediately ladle it over the sea bass and sprinkle on the toasted sunflower seeds.

Serves 4

This one has an Indonesian flavour and is somewhat on the spicy side. Sea bass is another tasty white fish available in local markets year-round.

I roast my own bell peppers on the barbecue (see page 148) but you can buy them by the jar already roasted.

SWEET BASIL HALIBUT
with peach and HONEYDEW SALSA

In the Pacific North-west where I live, fresh halibut (I don't like frozen) is avail-able in the summer and fall, which hap-pens to coincide nicely with the sea-son of peaches. If you prepare the Peach and Honeydew Salsa the day before, you can have this entrée on the table in an hour – most of which is marinating time.

4	halibut steaks, 1 inch thick
2 tbsp	black pepper
1/4 cup	olive oil
4	garlic cloves, minced fine
2 tbsp	fresh basil, minced fine

Sprinkle both sides of the steaks liberally with the black pepper and place in a glass dish.

Prepare a marinade by blending the olive oil, garlic and basil in a blender for 2 to 3 minutes on a high speed. Pour over the steaks and refrigerate for 30 to 45 minutes. Gently turn the steaks several times during the marinating period.

Discard the marinade and place the steaks on an oiled grid in a preheated barbecue. Grill over a medium to high heat (350 to 400°F) for 5 to 8 minutes a side, or until the fish just tends to flake. Using a wide spatula, turn the steaks once during the cooking period. Serve Peach and Honeydew Salsa as a sidedish.

Serves 4

Peach and honeydew salsa

1 cup	firm ripe peaches, peeled and diced
1 cup	ripe honeydew melon, peeled and diced
3 tbsp	fresh lime juice
1 tbsp	fresh mint, minced fine
1/2 tbsp	fresh ginger, grated fine
1/2 tbsp	sea salt

Combine all the ingredients in a glass bowl and allow to sit at room temperature until ready to serve. Toss gently before serving. Yields 2 cups.

halibut with
LEMON SHRIMP SAUCE

4	halibut steaks, ¾ inch thick
	extra virgin olive oil
½ lb	butter
2 tbsp	fresh lemon juice
½ tsp	balsamic vinegar
½ tsp	black pepper
¼ tsp	salt
¾ lb	fresh shrimp meat, minced

Halibut is probably the firmest-fleshed fish harvested from the ocean. Its firm texture makes it very easy to turn over on the barbecue. The lemon shrimp sauce adds delicate colour and the tang that halibut seems to need.

To prepare the shrimp sauce, melt the butter in a small saucepan and stir in the lemon juice, balsamic vinegar, black pepper and salt. When the mixture begins to bubble, remove it from the heat and stir in the shrimp meat. Cover with a lid and set aside.

Place the halibut steaks on an oiled grid over a medium to high heat (350 to 400°F). Grill for 6 to 8 minutes a side. Turn and baste with the olive oil several times.

Bring the shrimp sauce to a bubbling stage. Arrange the halibut steaks on a serving platter and spoon equal amounts of the sauce over each steak.

Serves 4

GRILLED SWORDFISH STEAKS

WITH AVOCADO AND LIME

My uncle – Barba Joe – has made this 24-hour marinade his specialty. Swordfish may at times during the fishing season acquire an iodine aroma and taste. This marinade masks that taste and enhances the flavour of the fish.

4	swordfish steaks, ¾ inch thick
¾ cup	olive oil
¼ cup	fresh lime juice
10	large garlic cloves, coarsely minced
1 tbsp	fresh ginger, grated
2	large avocados
½ cup	green onions
¼ cup	fresh cilantro

Place the swordfish steaks in a single layer in a glass dish.

Prepare a marinade by whisking the olive oil, lime juice, garlic and ginger in a bowl. Pour two thirds of this mixture over the steaks. Reserve the remainder.

Cover the steaks with food wrap and refrigerate for 8 to 24 hours. Turn them several times during the marinating period.

Before grilling the steaks, pit, skin and coarsely chop the avocados, coarsely chop the green onions and chop the fresh cilantro.

Place the steaks on the grid over a medium to high heat (350 to 400°F). Season with salt and pepper and grill for approximately 6 minutes a side. If you can, leave grid marks on the steaks for an attractive appearance. Remove the steaks from the barbecue and arrange on a large serving platter.

Bring the reserved marinade to a boil. Remove from the heat, quickly stir in the avocado and green onion. Allow to stand for a few minutes, just to heat the avocado. Ladle the sauce over the steaks and sprinkle with cilantro.

Serves 4

Korcula island
BLUEFIN tuna

4	tuna steaks, 1 inch thick
½ cup	orange juice
¼ cup	olive oil
¼ cup	fresh parsley, minced
3	garlic cloves, minced fine
3 tbsp	fresh lime juice
1 tbsp	black pepper
1 tbsp	soy sauce

Place the tuna steaks in a shallow glass dish.

Prepare a marinating/basting sauce by combining the remaining ingredients in a bowl. Pour the sauce over the steaks and allow to marinate at room temperature for 30 to 45 minutes. Turn the steaks several times during this period.

Grill the steaks in a preheated barbecue over a medium to high heat (350 to 400°F) for 5 minutes. Turn them and grill for an additional 3 minutes. Baste frequently with the sauce during the entire cooking time.

Serves 4

An adaptation of my Uncle Nick's recipe, direct from the island of Korcula, which is off the Dalmatian Coast of Croatia. At one time this area had one of the largest tuna and mackerel fisheries in southern Europe. The fresh taste of citrus always complements tuna.

MINT AND CITRUS TUNA STEAKS
with avocado and olive saltsa

If you have already prepared the Avocado and Olive Saltsa, this makes a quick, light entrée. The mint helps to mellow the strong taste of tuna. With the popularity of Japanese restaurants in the Pacific Northwest, we can buy fresh tuna year-round.

4	¾-lb tuna steaks
2 tbsp	brown sugar
1 tbsp	cornstarch
1 tbsp	fresh mint, minced
¼ tsp	sea salt
1 cup	orange juice
3 tbsp	fresh lime juice
2 tsp	lime zest, fresh grated

Blend the brown sugar, cornstarch, mint and sea salt in a small saucepan. Add the orange and lime juices, and bring to a low simmer. Stir in the lime zest and remove from the heat.

Grill the steaks over a medium to high heat (350 to 400°F) for approximately 5 to 7 minutes a side. Baste frequently with the citrus sauce during the entire cooking time.

Serves 4 to 6

Avocado and olive saltsa

3	medium avocados, pitted, peeled and coarsely chopped
½ cup	pitted black olives
½ cup	kalamata olives, halved and pitted
½ cup	pitted green olives
¾ cup	provolone cheese, in ½-inch cubes
⅓ cup	olive oil
½ cup	fresh lime juice
2 tbsp	sugar
¼ tsp	dried and crushed red chilies
¼ tsp	cumin powder

That is not a spelling mistake. Saltsa is a eastern European term for relishes. This is my slight variation on a Dalmatian favourite, which is worth the long marinating time.

Place the avocado, olives and cheese in a large glass bowl.

Combine the remaining ingredients in a glass jar, cover with a lid and shake well. Pour over the avocados, olives and cheese and refrigerate for 6 to 24 hours. Toss gently during the marinating period.

Allow to stand at room temperature for an hour before serving.

Serves 4 to 6

SIMPLY GRILLED TUNA STEAKS WITH LIME-ZEST SPINACH

4	tuna steaks
3 tbsp	olive oil
2 tbsp	fresh lime juice
3	large garlic cloves, minced fine
1 tbsp	paprika
2 tsp	fresh cilantro, minced fine
2 tsp	black pepper
½ tsp	salt

Sometimes the tuna we buy is actually skipjack, a related fish that can have an overwhelming flavour. For this reason, I lightly marinate tuna most of the time. You can have this meal on the table in 30 minutes.

Place the tuna steaks in a shallow glass dish. Add the olive oil and lime juice and allow to sit at room temperature for 20 minutes. Turn the steaks several times during this period.

Combine the garlic, paprika, cilantro, pepper and salt in a bowl. Remove the steaks from the oil, pat dry and rub well with this dry spice mixture, using it all.

Grill the steaks over a high heat (400°F) to a rare to medium doneness. This will take approximately 6 minutes a side.

Arrange the steaks on a large serving platter. Toss the spinach, placing equal amounts on top of each steak and serve.

Lime-zest spinach

1 bunch	spinach, rinsed, trimmed and chopped
1 bunch	fresh parsley, chopped
⅓ cup	extra virgin olive oil
1	medium garlic clove, minced very fine
½ tbsp	balsamic vinegar
½ tsp	lime zest, grated

Combine all the ingredients in a glass bowl. Set aside and allow to stand at room temperature for no more than 20 minutes before using.

Serves 4

KABOBS
of SHELLFISH

Save some work before dinner by preparing the Tartar Sauce the day before. The lobster, prawns and scallops make a great combination. You will also notice that when lobster is barbecued it will be more flavourful than when it is steamed or boiled.

2	½-lb fresh or defrosted frozen lobster tails
8	large fresh prawns, peeled with the tails on
8	large fresh scallops
8	large pimiento-stuffed green olives
16	cherry tomatoes
¼ cup	butter
2 tbsp	fresh lime juice
1 tsp	black pepper

Remove the meat from the lobster tails and cut each tail into 8 equal pieces.

Thread 8 skewers in this order: lobster, tomato, prawn, olive, scallop, tomato and lobster. To prevent the vegetables from spinning, use two parallel skewers about ¼ to ½ inch apart.

Melt the butter in a small saucepan and stir in the lime juice and black pepper.

Grill the skewers over a medium heat (350°F) until done, approximately 9 to 12 minutes. Turn and baste with the butter mixture several times during the cooking period. Serve with Tartar Sauce.

Serves 4

Tartar Sauce

¾ cup	mayonnaise
1 tbsp	sweet pickles, minced
1 tbsp	onion, grated
1 tsp	fresh parsley, minced fine
½ tsp	hot sauce (e.g., Melinda's XXXtra Hot Sauce)

Combine all the ingredients in a glass bowl and refrigerate overnight. Allow the sauce to reach room temperature before serving.

Yields ¾ cup

LOBSTER, PEACHES AND NECTARINES WITH AN
APRICOT GLAZE

2 large fresh or defrosted frozen lobster tails

2 firm peaches, peeled and each cut into 4 cubes

2 firm nectarines, peeled and each cut into 4 cubes

2 tbsp butter

¼ cup canned apricots, puréed

¼ cup Madeira

2 garlic cloves, minced fine

¼ tsp black pepper

¼ tsp salt

Now, this is seasonal! A summertime combination of lobster, peaches and nectarines, basted with a Madeira wine and apricot sauce.

Remove the meat from the lobster tails, cut each one into 12 cubes and set aside.

To prepare a basting sauce, melt the butter in a small saucepan and stir in the puréed apricots, Madeira and spices. Simmer for 3 minutes and set aside.

On each of 8 skewers thread the cubed fish and fruit in this order: lobster, peach, lobster, nectarine and lobster. To prevent the fruit from spinning, use two parallel skewers about ¼ to ½ inch apart.

Grill the kabobs over a medium to high heat (350 to 400°F) for approximately 5 to 8 minutes a side. Turn and baste continually with the sauce.

Serves 4

HOT BARBECUE
Dungeness CRAB

Grilled or roasted crab is more succulent than boiled. The flavour of the crab intensifies on the grill.

If you intend to do some crabbing at the beach, prepare the basting sauce and the shrimp sauce at home. Take them with you in a cooler on ice. When you catch one of those eight-legged creatures, grasp it firmly where the legs are attached, and break the top shell in half against a sharp rock. Remove the shell, discard the innards and rinse the crab well in the ocean (feeding the seagulls). Grill it on a hibachi or portable gas barbecue.

2	large live Dungeness crab
1 lb	butter
3 tbsp	sweet hot sauce (e.g., Tiger Sauce)
2 tbsp	fresh lime juice
1/2 tbsp	Worcestershire sauce
1/4 tsp	salt
1/2 lb	fresh shrimp meat

Purchase live crabs at your local fish market. Have the fishmonger cut the crabs in half, remove the shells and clean out the interiors. Take the crabs directly home and keep refrigerated until ready for use.

To prepare a basting sauce, melt the butter in a saucepan. Stir in the sweet hot sauce, lime juice, Worcestershire and salt. Cook only until warmed and then remove from the heat.

To prepare the shrimp sauce, put half of the basting sauce in a food processor. Add the shrimp meat and purée. Transfer to a small saucepan.

Keep these two sauces separate, on very low heats, just enough to keep them warm.

Place the crabs, body meat facing up, on the grid. Grill over a high heat (400°F) for 10 minutes. Lower the heat to medium (300 to 350°F) and grill for 10 to 15 minutes more. Baste with the butter sauce until it is all used.

Place half a crab on each dinner plate. Serve the heated shrimp sauce in individual dipping bowls.

Serves 4

MAPLE SYRUP
BARBECUE PRAWNS

24	large fresh prawns, peeled and the tails left intact
½ cup	maple syrup
1 tbsp	raspberry vinegar
½ tsp	HP Sauce
½ tsp	mustard powder
15	large garlic cloves

Place the prawns in one layer in a glass dish.

To prepare a basting sauce, combine the maple syrup, raspberry vinegar, HP sauce and mustard powder in a bowl. Using a garlic press, press five peeled garlic cloves and add to the marinade, blending well. Pour half of this mixture over the prawns and allow to stand at room temperature for 30 to 45 minutes. Put the remainder in a saucepan and keep warm.

In a small saucepan cover the remaining garlic cloves with water and simmer just until they begin to get tender, 3 to 5 minutes. Remove their skins and set aside.

Alternate the prawns and garlic on 4 skewers. To prevent the garlic from spinning, use two parallel skewers about ¼ inch apart.

Grill over a medium to high heat (350 to 400°F) for approximately 6 to 8 minutes. Turn and baste the prawns with the sauce until done.

Bring the reserved basting sauce to a low simmer, transfer to a gravy boat and serve with the prawns.

Serves 2

Once in a Las Vegas hotel I ordered prawns from room service, and they sent up an order of prunes. That's how I learned that where we serve prawns, many people serve large or extra-large shrimp. The maple syrup gives these prawns a Canadian touch.

ADRIATIC
hot garlic prawns

This is an adaptation of a prawn dish my father used to make. It's a romantic recipe – just enough prawns for the two of you. Eat them for dinner or, if the mood strikes, as a mid-day snack.

12	large fresh prawns, heads removed
1/4 cup	olive oil
1/4 cup	fresh lime juice
8	large garlic cloves
2 tbsp	hot sauce (e.g., Melinda's XXXtra Hot Sauce)
1 tsp	black pepper
1/2 tsp	salt

From the belly side, cut the prawns in half lengthwise to the shell, but not through. Rinse in cold water and place them cut side down in a shallow glass dish. Using the back of your hand, press them down firmly to open and flatten them.

To prepare a basting sauce, put the garlic cloves through a garlic press before combining them with the remaining ingredients in a glass bowl. Pour half of this mixture over the prawns and refrigerate for 30 to 45 minutes. Put the remainder in a saucepan and keep warm.

Place the prawns, spread open, on the grid, over a high heat (400°F). Grill for approximately 8 minutes, turning only once. Baste the prawns with the marinating sauce several times during the grilling period.

Arrange the prawns in a shallow serving dish. Heat the reserved sauce, spoon it over top and sprinkle with pepper and salt.

Serves 2

skewered halibut
CHEEKS

10	medium halibut cheeks, cut in half
20	large fresh prawns, heads and shells removed, tails intact
10	cherry tomatoes
1/3 cup	orange marmalade
1/2 cup	olive oil
1/4 cup	fresh parsley, minced
6	large garlic cloves, minced fine
2 tbsp	grainy Dijon mustard
2 tbsp	sweet hot sauce (e.g., Tiger Sauce)
1/2 tbsp	cumin powder

I consider the cheeks to be the filet mignon of the halibut. And so apparently do other people because they are quickly bought up during the fishing season. Most people would be satisfied eating three cheeks.

Prepare the marmalade sauce by whisking together the marmalade, olive oil, parsley, garlic, mustard, hot sauce and cumin in a large bowl. Add the prawns and halibut cheeks, tossing well to coat the seafood.

Thread 2 prawns, 2 pieces of halibut and a tomato on each of 10 skewers. To prevent the halibut cheeks and tomatoes from spinning, use two parallel skewers about 1/4 to 1/2 inch apart.

Grill over a medium to high heat (350 to 400°F) for approximately 4 minutes a side. Baste gently with some of the marmalade sauce while doing so.

Arrange the skewers on a serving platter. Heat any remaining marmalade sauce and drizzle over the kabobs. Serve immediately.

Serves 4

with a marmalade glaze

STEAMED
prawn pockets WITH YUKON GOLD POTATOES

The yellow-fleshed Yukon potato is delicious and stays firm during any type of cooking. Add a salad and you have an easy dinner.

20	large fresh prawns, heads and shells removed
4	medium Yukon gold potatoes, sliced ¼ inch thick
1 cup	leeks, minced
1 cup	plum tomatoes, sliced very thin
2	fresh limes
8 tbsp	butter
2 tsp	dill weed, crushed
1 tsp	dried whole Mexican oregano
	salt
	black pepper

Place the prawns, potatoes, leeks and tomatoes in a glass bowl. Squeeze the juice of the two limes over the top and set aside for 5 minutes.

Have 4 large pieces of heavy-duty aluminum foil on a large work area. Place 1 tablespoon of butter in the centre of each one.

Arrange the potatoes over and around the butter, overlapping each slice. Distribute the minced leeks equally over the potatoes. Put 5 prawns on top. Finish off by distributing equal amounts of tomato over each. Sprinkle with dill weed, oregano, salt and pepper. Dot each one with another tablespoon of butter.

Fold the aluminum foil around the food and crimp the edges to seal. Place on the barbecue, over a medium to high heat (350 to 400°F), and steam for 25 to 35 minutes.

Transfer the wrapped dinners to individual, shallow bowls and serve.

Serves 4

A medley of
GRILLED SEAFOOD

12	fresh mussels, shucked
12	fresh clams, shucked
12	sea scallops, shucked
12	large fresh prawns, heads removed
2	fresh or defrosted frozen lobster tails
1 cup	pink grapefruit juice
1 cup	orange juice
1/2 cup	fresh lemon juice
3 tbsp	molasses
1/4 cup	fresh parsley, minced fine
	black pepper
1 tsp	sugar
1	large lemon

A seafood-for-all-seasons combination, enhanced with a short, fruity marinating session. All you need with this one is some freshly baked sourdough bread.

Remove the meat from the lobster tails, cut into 1-inch cubes and place in a large glass bowl. Add the remaining seafood, the fruit juices and the molasses to the bowl and allow to sit at room temperature for at least 30 to 45 minutes. Toss often during this period.

Drain the seafood, reserving the juices. Place the seafood on a grill grid that prevents smaller items from falling into the fire, and grill over a medium to high heat (350 to 400°F) for 8 to 10 minutes. Turn and baste with the fruit juices often during the cooking time.

Arrange the seafood on a large serving platter. Sprinkle with the parsley, black pepper and sugar. Squeeze the juice of a lemon over the top and serve.

Serves 4

DALMATIAN BARBECUE SQUID
stuffed with shrimp and garlic

Papa's creation from Croatia. Squid are most often found in the freezer section of your fish market. When I have the opportunity, I purchase them fresh. A variety of grilled peppers, a fresh green salad and baguette bread complete this meal.

20	small squid bodies, cleaned and with the outer membrane left on
1/4 lb	shrimp meat, minced fine
3 tbsp	fine bread crumbs
2 tbsp	green onions, minced fine
1 tbsp	olive oil
1/2 tbsp	black pepper
1/4 cup	olive oil
4	garlic cloves, minced fine
3 tbsp	fresh parsley, minced

Combine the shrimp meat, bread crumbs, green onions, 1 tablespoon of olive oil and the black pepper in a bowl.

Stuff equal amounts of the shrimp mixture loosely into each squid body. Do not overstuff as squid have a high water content which makes them shrink when cooked. If they are overstuffed, they will split open. When the squid are stuffed, cook immediately or refrigerate until ready for use.

Prepare a basting sauce by combining the olive oil, garlic and parsley in a bowl.

Grill the squid over a low to medium heat (250 to 350°F) for approximately 15 minutes. Roll them up and down the grid to cook all over. Baste with the sauce often. Turn the heat to high and grill the squid until they are slightly charred on all sides.

Make a slight slit, lengthwise, on the squid. Baste any remaining sauce into the slits. Turn the heat off, close the lid and allow to sit for 2 minutes before serving.

Serves 4

adriatic squid
STEAKS

4	4-oz squid steaks
1/3 cup	olive oil
1/4 cup	fresh parsley, minced
6	large garlic cloves, minced fine
2 tbsp	fresh lime juice

Make slashes in the steaks, approximately a quarter of the way through the meat. Do this diagonally, both ways, to create a diamond effect on the surface. Place the steaks in a glass dish in a single layer.

Combine the olive oil, parsley, garlic and lime juice in a bowl, pour over the squid steaks and allow to stand at room temperature for at least half an hour. Flip the steaks over a couple of times during this period.

Grill the steaks over a high heat (400°F) for 3 minutes a side, or until cooked through and grid marks appear on the surface. Serve with Spiced Tartar Sauce.

Serves 2

Prepare the tartar sauce the day before, and you'll have a 30-minute dinner solution. These steaks are great as a main course, accompanied by boiled potatoes and a fresh tomato salad. A wonderful change from the North American-influenced, deep-fried squid we so often see.

Spiced tartar sauce

1/2 cup	mayonnaise
2 tbsp	fresh lime juice
1 tbsp	Tabasco
1 tbsp	sweet pickles, minced fine
1 tbsp	green onions, minced
1 tsp	onion, grated
1 tsp	fresh parsley, minced

Combine all the ingredients in a glass bowl, cover with a lid and refrigerate overnight.

Yields 1/2 cup

WINE-BUTTERED
TROUT

I started cooking trout like this over a campfire when my children were young. The skin gets crispy, and my kids ate it like candy.

4	1 ½-lb fresh trout, cleaned and scaled
	black pepper
½ cup	butter
¼ cup	white wine
2 tbsp	cider vinegar
2 tbsp	brown sugar
1 tbsp	onion, grated
1	small garlic clove, minced fine
1 tsp	salt
1 tsp	paprika
1 tsp	hot sauce (e.g., Melinda's XXXtra Hot Sauce)

Entering in the belly, cut through the trouts' backbones but not through the skin. (A serrated knife works well.) This will allow you to open the fish and lay them flat in a long-handled fish basket. Sprinkle the meat side with the black pepper.

Prepare a basting sauce by combining the remaining ingredients in a saucepan and simmering for 10 minutes.

Grill the trout over a medium heat (350°F) for 10 to 15 minutes. Turn four times and baste liberally with the sauce. Sprinkle the meat side again with the black pepper and serve.

Serves 4

GRILLED BEEF AND PORK

EVEN THOUGH THEY ARE probably the most popular backyard barbecue food, I haven't given recipes for simple steaks. Nothing could be easier than throwing a steak on the grill. If Pat and I are eating alone, we'll share an eight-ounce filet mignon or a nice T-bone (Pat gets the filet and I eat the other side). I simply sprinkle the meat with salt and pepper and grill it to our taste, which is medium rare. My T-bone Steak with Tomato Baguette Bread is the simplest steak recipe you'll find in this book.

Pat and I eat hamburgers quite often, but I haven't included a recipe because my standard hamburger is also simple: a half pound of lean ground beef mixed with three finely chopped green onions and a teaspoon of barbecue sauce. No salt and pepper. Make two half-inch-thick patties. Grill them until they are charred on the outside. They will be cooked to the medium stage inside. That's the way we've always eaten our hamburgers, but these days it's prudent to cook ground beef until there is no red meat showing.

Despite the current concern about thoroughly cooking hamburgers, one of the most important factors in success-fully barbecuing meat is not to dry it out by overcooking. Several of my beef recipes use flank steak, a cut of meat that will be tough if it's overcooked but tender and juicy if done to the medium-rare stage.

Beef or pork ribs taste better when barbecued, grilled or baked slowly at low temperatures. Slower cooking is also better for you as it gets rid of more fat. The process will take from two to three hours at 200 to 250°F.

GRILLED BEEF AND PORK

Always remove the membrane from the bone side of ribs to allow the spices, heat and smoke to penetrate evenly and produce a more tender, tasty rib. To ensure that the meat pulls away from the bone easily, pierce both sides of each bone several times with a fork before cooking.

Metal rib racks hold ribs upright so you can fit more in your barbecue at one time. To achieve the same economy of space, roll the ribs into a loose jelly roll secured with a skewer. You can then stand them upright on the grid. Half an hour before they're done, unroll the ribs and baste with a barbecue sauce. Make a pile of the racks and rotate them within the pile a few times.

The test for doneness is simple: pull the end bone; if it doesn't come off easily, keep on cooking.

I've said these things before but they bear repeating: salting and spicing meat before cooking will enhance the flavour but not affect the juiciness. Don't wash meat before cooking; water will leach out the juices. Never thaw meat in a microwave; some areas will get cooked. And don't par-boil ribs unless you want to make rib soup.

BEEF TENDERLOIN WITH
FEVERISH
CUBAN DIPPING SAUCE

1	4-lb beef tenderloin, trimmed of fat and sinew
1/2 cup	olive oil
1/2 cup	grainy Dijon mustard
4	habanero chili peppers, seeded and chopped
4	large garlic cloves, chopped
1/4 cup	fresh lime juice
2 tbsp	vinegar
2 tbsp	balsamic vinegar
2 tbsp	fresh rosemary, minced
	fresh parsley

This is not a last-minute meal. After a 12- to 24-hour marinating, the tenderloin cooks at a lower heat and for a longer time than usual in fast grilling.

Wear latex gloves to protect your hands from the oil of the chilies while you seed and chop them and don't touch your face or eyes while working with the chilies. To prepare a marinade, purée the olive oil, mustard, chili peppers, garlic, lime juice, vinegars and rosemary in a food processor or blender.

Place the tenderloin in a glass dish and pour half the marinade over top. Keep the remainder under refrigeration. Cover the tenderloin with food wrap and refrigerate for 12 to 24 hours, turning it several times during the marinating period.

Remove the tenderloin from the marinade and wipe with a paper towel. Preheat the barbecue to 250 to 300°F and put the tenderloin on the grid 6 to 8 inches from the coals or the burner.

Barbecue at this temperature for 1 to 2 hours. Turn the tenderloin and baste it with the marinade several times while it cooks. When the internal temperature reaches 130°F (for rare meat), transfer the tenderloin to a cutting board. Cover it with food wrap and allow to stand for 10 minutes.

Bring the reserved marinade to a boil in a small saucepan. Ladle it into a glass dipping bowl and put the bowl in the centre of a large serving platter.

Slice the meat across the grain and arrange the slices around the dipping sauce. Garnish with parsley sprigs.

Serves 6

NEW YORK
STEAKS WITH PINEAPPLE CHILI SAUCE

To get dinner on the table faster, make the pineapple chili sauce the day before. While the steaks are marinating, put a sweet potato in the oven at 350°F. In 20 to 25 minutes, take it from the oven, peel and slice it and season with salt and pepper. Put the slices on the grill and baste with oil.

4	6-oz New York steaks, 1 inch thick
½	fresh pineapple, peeled and cored
3	dried ancho chilies, stemmed and seeded
1 cup	hot water
½ cup	green onions, green ends only, minced
1 tbsp	fresh cilantro, minced fine
½ tsp	cayenne pepper

To prepare a basting sauce, cut the pineapple into chunks and purée in a food processor. Transfer the purée to a bowl. Grill or broil the ancho chilies until softened. Add the water and anchos to the food processor and process until smooth. Strain the ancho purée through a fine sieve and blend it with the green onions, cilantro, cayenne pepper and the puréed pineapple.

Place the steaks in a shallow glass dish. Pour half of the basting sauce over them and put the remainder in a small saucepan. Allow the steaks to stand at room temperature for half an hour or more. Turn them several times to coat them with the sauce.

Pat the steaks dry with paper towels before putting them on the grid of a preheated barbecue. Grill them over a medium to high heat (350 to 400°F) for 5 to 7 minutes a side. Turn several times and baste often with the sauce.

When the steaks are nearly done, bring the remaining basting sauce to a simmer. Place it in individual dipping bowls and serve along with the steaks.

Serves 4

Texas Beef Brisket, p.46

Barbecue FILLET
steaks crusted with cheese

4	6-oz beef tenderloin steaks
	meat seasoning spice rub (any on page 26)
¼ lb	butter
¼ cup	fine bread crumbs
¼ cup	Swiss cheese, grated
½ tbsp	black pepper
1 doz	white nugget potatoes
1	medium red bell pepper
1	medium yellow bell pepper
1	medium green bell pepper

This is an all-inclusive meal; cooking dinner can't get much easier. The cheese and butter coating really tops off this wonderful steak. Prepare the topping a day ahead or in time to allow it to chill enough to slice.

Bring the butter to room temperature in a bowl. Stir in the bread crumbs, cheese and black pepper, blending well. On a piece of wax paper, roll this mixture out into a log approximately 2 inches in diameter. Wrap the log in wax paper and refrigerate overnight or until cold enough to slice.

Before beginning to cook the steaks, parboil the potatoes. Seed the peppers and slice them in ½-inch rings.

Sprinkle each side of the steaks liberally with your favourite meat seasoning and rub it well into the meat.

Put the steaks on one side of a preheated barbecue and the vegetables on the other. Brush the vegetables with oil. Grill the steaks and vegetables over a medium to high heat (350 to 400°F) until the steaks are medium-rare. Turn the steaks several times and the vegetables often during the cooking period.

Cut the butter log into four equal rounds. Put one round on top of each steak. Close the lid and grill briefly until the topping turns a golden brown and begins to form a crust. Arrange the steaks on a serving platter and surround them with the grilled vegetables.

Serves 4

Pork Tenderloin with Mustard, Lemon and Rosemary, p. 112
Balsamic Grilled Fruits, p. 168

HERO OF HEROES

with onions, tomatoes and cucumber

My improved submarine sandwich. Slicing the meat very thinly will release more flavour to blend with the vegetables. For a hands-on, informal dinner, serve Hot Corn on the Cob (see page 151).

1	3-lb fillet of beef
¼ cup	olive oil
¼ cup	butter, melted
2	loaves baguette bread, cut in half lengthwise
2	red onions, sliced very thin
4	plum tomatoes, sliced very thin
1	large English cucumber, sliced very thin
	salt
	black pepper

Combine the olive oil and butter in a bowl and set aside.

Put the steak on the grid of a preheated barbecue and grill it over a medium to high heat (350 to 400°F) for approximately 35 minutes. Turn and baste often with some of the olive oil and butter mixture. This will produce a rare to medium fillet.

Remove the steak to a cutting board, sprinkle with salt and pepper and loosely tent with food wrap while you distribute the onions, tomatoes and cucumber on the bottom halves of the bread.

Slice the fillet very thinly across the grain and arrange the slices on top of the vegetables.

Brush the top halves of the bread with the remaining mixture of olive oil and butter, sprinkle with salt and pepper and put them on top of the sandwiches. Slice the sandwiches crosswise in 4-inch-wide slices.

Serves 4 to 6

TEXAS FAJITAS
– the real thing

4   ½-lb skirt steaks
2 tbsp   fajita dry spice seasoning
2   large red bell peppers, halved and seeded
1   green bell pepper, halved and seeded
1   large onion, quartered
1 sprig   fresh cilantro, minced fine
1 tsp   fresh lime juice
1 tbsp   olive oil
4   10-inch, flour tortillas
     sour cream
     guacamole, purchased
     fresh salsa, purchased

Authentic southern Texas fajitas call for skirt steak cooked on the barbecue (not sliced round steak sautéed in a wok). You may have to order skirt steak from your butcher. If you can't find it, substitute a thin flank steak. You'll get the best results if the meat is slightly charred on the outside and rare to medium inside. Serve fajitas with A Hot Mexican Fiesta of Vegetables (page 160).

Sprinkle half the fajita seasoning on the bottom of a shallow glass dish. Place the steaks on top and sprinkle them with the remainder of the seasoning. Cover the steaks with food wrap and refrigerate for at least 2 or up to 24 hours. Bring to room temperature before cooking.

When you are ready to begin cooking, push toothpicks through the onion quarters to hold them together. Arrange them and the bell peppers on the preheated barbecue and grill over a medium to high heat (350 to 400°F). Turn the vegetables frequently, cooking them until they just begin to char.

Remove the vegetables from the barbecue, extract the toothpicks and put the onions and the bell peppers in a plastic bag that zips closed. Add the cilantro, lime juice and olive oil. Seal the bag, shake well and set aside.

Grill the steaks directly above the heat for 3 to 5 minutes a side. Remove them to a cutting board and slice them thinly across the grain. Transfer the meat to the centre of a serving platter. Coarsely chop all the vegetables and arrange them around the outside of the platter, encircling the meat.

The rest is up to your guests. Invite them to spread some sour cream on one half of a tortilla and guacamole on the other half. Lay some meat and vegetables across the centre. Dab some fresh salsa on top. Fold the tortilla over top, bring in the sides and roll it up. Serves 4

SIZZLING BEEF Malaysia
with peanut dipping sauce

An East-meets-West dish, with a variation on the traditional peanut sauce achieved by adding a few southwestern U.S. flavours.

2	¾-lb flank steaks
3 oz	grapefruit juice
3 oz	orange juice
3 tbsp	fresh lime juice
1 tsp	cumin powder
1 tsp	coriander powder
1 tsp	salt
½ tsp	cayenne pepper

Slice the steak very thin across the grain. Place the steak strips in a glass dish. Combine the juices and spices in a bowl and pour the mixture over the steak strips. Allow them to stand at room temperature for half an hour or more. Turn the strips occasionally during the marinating period.

Pat the strips dry and thread them on 16 skewers in accordion folds, pushing the folds close together which will help to keep the meat from overcooking. Grill on a preheated barbecue over a medium to high heat (350 to 400°F) until done, approximately 5 to 8 minutes. Serve with Peanut Dipping Sauce.

Serves 4 to 6

Peanut dipping sauce

⅓ cup	salted peanuts
2 tbsp	olive oil
1	small onion, chopped
1	tomato, peeled and chopped
2	large garlic cloves, chopped
2 oz	pineapple juice
3 tbsp	sweet hot sauce (e.g., Tiger Sauce)
1 tbsp	fresh lime juice
1 tbsp	dried and crushed red chilies
1 tbsp	soy sauce
2 tsp	molasses
1 tsp	lime zest, fresh grated
½ tsp	cumin powder

Grind the peanuts in a food processor. Add the remaining ingredients to the food processor and blend them thoroughly. Transfer the mixture to a small saucepan and simmer until slightly thickened. Ladle the heated sauce into individual dipping bowls.

Yields 1 cup

FLANK STEAK SALAD

1	¾-lb flank steak
1 tbsp	meat seasoning spice rub (any on page 26)
2 cups	arugula, torn into bite-size pieces
2	large avocados, pitted, peeled and diced
2	large plum tomatoes, diced
1	large Belgium endive, torn into bite-size pieces
½ cup	Monterey Jack cheese, grated
¼ cup	pine nuts, toasted
⅓ cup	olive oil
2 tbsp	raspberry vinegar
1 tbsp	fresh lime juice
1 tbsp	hot sauce
½ tsp	black pepper
¼ tsp	salt

I created this dish to solve a perennial firehall problem – being interrupted by the fire bell just as we're sitting down to eat. We hate coming back to cold pasta, but this salad holds well at any stage of its preparation. Slightly char the outside of the steak, leaving it medium-cooked on the inside.

Using the blunt edge of a heavy cleaver, pound the steak across the grain, flattening it slightly and just breaking the surface of the meat. Rub the entire steak with your favourite meat seasoning spice.

Place the steak on the grid of a preheated barbecue and grill it over a medium to high heat (350 to 400°F) until both sides are browned and slightly charred and the inside is at the medium stage. This will take about 6 minutes a side.

Slice the steak across the grain into very thin strips. Put the strips in a bowl and set aside.

Toss the arugula, avocado, tomato and Belgium endive in a glass salad bowl. Add the flank steak and toss gently. Sprinkle with the grated cheese and toasted pine nuts and set aside.

Combine the olive oil, vinegar, lime juice, hot sauce, pepper and salt in a glass jar. Cover with a lid and shake well. Drizzle over the salad and hope the fire bell doesn't ring.

Serves 4

HONEY-AND-MUSTARD
GLAZED steak
AND CARAMELIZED ONIONS

To make this into a meal cooked entirely on the barbecue, I would do bunches of 6 to 8 asparagus stalks (tied together with butcher's twine, brushed with oil and grilled for 8 to 10 minutes) and red or yellow bell peppers (cut into halves, brushed with oil and grilled for 10 to 15 minutes). On the side element of the barbecue, I'd boil potatoes and serve them plain.

2	6-oz New York steaks, 1 inch thick
1	large onion, quartered
	salt
	black pepper
1/4 cup	Dijon mustard
2 tbsp	liquid honey
1 tbsp	sweet hot sauce (e.g., Tiger Sauce)
1 tsp	cider vinegar
1 tsp	water

Salt and pepper the steaks and set them aside.

Push toothpicks through the quarter sections of onion to hold them together.

To prepare the glaze, blend the mustard, honey, hot sauce, vinegar and water in a bowl.

Put the steaks and onions on the grid of a preheated barbecue and grill them over a medium to high heat (350 to 400°F) for 10 to 14 minutes. Turn and baste often with the glaze.

Serves 2

Filets MIGNONS
with grilled papaya

4	8-oz filets mignons, 1 inch thick
4	large papaya slices, ¾ inch thick
3 tbsp	olive oil
1 tsp	balsamic vinegar
1	large garlic clove, minced fine
1 tsp	black pepper
½ tsp	salt
1	large lime, quartered

This recipe has one of my favourite flavours – balsamic vinegar – and a fruit I like very much – papaya. It seems to me that steak and papaya make a great combination. This has the added advantage of a short marinating period.

Prepare a marinade and basting sauce by combining the olive oil, vinegar, garlic, black pepper and salt in a glass jar. Cover with a lid and shake well. Pour two-thirds of the sauce over the steaks in a shallow glass dish and put the remainder in a small saucepan.

Allow the steaks to stand at room temperature for half an hour or more. Turn the steaks several times during this period.

Pat the steaks dry with paper towels and put them on the grid of a preheated barbecue. Grill them over a medium heat (350°F) for a total time of 8 to 10 minutes. Turn and baste often with the marinade.

Five minutes after you begin cooking the steaks, put the slices of papaya on the barbecue. Grill until lightly browned.

Put the steaks on dinner plates. Bring the remaining sauce in the saucepan to a low simmer and drizzle it over the steaks. Put a slice of papaya on top of each steak and squeeze the juice of a quarter of a lime over each serving.

Serves 4

T-BONE steak

with tomato baguette bread

Now this is quick and basic, a simple, traditional steak, with the addition of the tomato baguette bread to give it a contemporary accent. Serve a hearty, plain salad, and you have a meal.

2	12-oz T-bone steaks, ¾ inch thick
	meat seasoning spice rub (any on page 26)
4 tbsp	olive oil
2	garlic cloves, minced fine
½ loaf	baguette bread, cut in half, lengthwise
4	plum tomatoes, halved
3 tbsp	Parmesan cheese, freshly grated

Combine the olive oil and garlic in a glass bowl.

Season the steaks with your favourite spices and put them on the grid of a preheated barbecue. Grill over a medium heat (350°F) for 10 to 15 minutes. Turn and baste with the olive oil mixture often.

Brush the cut side of the bread with the olive oil mixture. About 5 minutes before the steaks are done, place the bread on the barbecue with the cut side down and grill until lightly toasted. Turn the bread over and add the halved tomatoes to the barbecue. Brush the bread and tomatoes with olive oil and grill for several minutes.

Arrange the tomatoes on the baguette and sprinkle with the Parmesan cheese. Close the lid and cook the bread and steaks for 2 to 3 minutes more.

Serves 2

HOT TERIYAKI STRIPS

1	2-lb flank steak
¼ cup	beef consommé
¼ cup	hot sauce (e.g., Melinda's XXXtra Hot Sauce)
¼ cup	green onions, minced fine
3 tbsp	fresh lime juice
2 tbsp	soy sauce
2 tbsp	liquid honey
2 tsp	black pepper

The long marinating gives this dish its Japanese taste. The avocado will mellow the heat and the lime will cleanse your palate, bringing out the many flavours of this dish. Don't overdo the cooking; you want the steak rare to medium.

Slice the steak across the grain in ⅛-inch strips. Place the strips of flank steak in a glass bowl. Prepare a marinade by combining the remaining ingredients in a bowl. Pour the mixture over the meat and refrigerate for 12 to 24 hours. Stir the strips several times during the marinating period.

Before grilling, let the strips come to room temperature, dry them with paper towels and place them in a long-handled, hinged broiler. Grill in a preheated barbecue over a high heat (400°F) for approximately 10 minutes. Shake the broiler and baste frequently with any remaining marinade.

Serve over a platter of brown rice and with a side dish of Avocado with Lime Wedges.

Avocado with lime wedges

4	large avocados, chilled
2	limes, unpeeled and cut into wedges
	salt

Cut the avocados in half lengthwise. Remove the pit and insert 2 wedges of lime into each hole. Arrange the avocados on a large platter. Invite your guests to squeeze lime juice over the avocado, sprinkle it with salt and eat it with a spoon.

Serves 4 to 6

FLANK STEAK WITH GRAINY Dijon

If you like Dijon, you will love this recipe. Cooking the steak to a rare to medium stage will retain its juices, which will mellow the bite of the mustard and vinegars.

1	1-lb flank steak
½ cup	olive oil
3 tbsp	grainy Dijon mustard
2 tbsp	white wine vinegar
1 tbsp	balsamic vinegar
¼ tsp	white pepper

Place the flank steak in a shallow glass dish. Prepare a basting sauce by blending the oil, mustard, vinegars and pepper in a bowl. Pour the sauce over the steak, cover and allow to stand at room temperature for half an hour or more. Turn the steak several times during this period.

Pat the steak dry with paper towels and put it on the grid of a preheated barbecue and grill over a high heat (400°F) for 5 minutes a side, searing it well. Bring the marinade to a simmer on the side element of the barbecue. Lower the heat to medium (350°F) and grill the steak for an additional 8 to 10 minutes. Turn and baste with the warmed marinade frequently.

Transfer the steak to a large platter, cover with food wrap and allow to stand for 5 minutes. Slice across the grain into very thin strips and serve with its own juices. Rather than slicing this steak on a board and then placing the slices on a serving platter, I slice directly on a stainless steel platter so that the juices are not lost.

Serves 2

INDIAN
FLANK STEAK with Cuban spice sauce

1	2-lb flank steak
2 tbsp	black pepper
½ cup	fresh lime juice
1 tsp	coriander powder
½ tsp	turmeric powder
½ tsp	chili powder
½ tsp	salt

Because flank steak is a versatile cut of meat, it's used extensively in barbecue. For the best results, these steaks should usually be slightly charred on the outside and cooked until rare to medium on the inside. The marinating time is 12 to 24 hours.

Rub the entire flank steak with the black pepper and place it in a shallow glass dish. Put the remaining ingredients in a glass jar, shake well and pour over the steak. Refrigerate for 12 to 24 hours. Turn the steak several times during the marinating period.

Pat the steak dry with paper towels. Grill the steak in a preheated barbecue over medium to high heat (350 to 400°F) for 6 to 8 minutes a side. Turn and baste often with the marinade. This will produce a rare to medium steak. Slice very thinly, across the grain, and serve with your favourite dipping sauce or Cuban Spice Sauce.

Serves 4

Cuban spice sauce

4	habanero chili peppers
3 to 4	serrano chili peppers
2 tbsp	fresh lime juice
1 tbsp	vinegar
1 tbsp	fresh cilantro, chopped
½ tbsp	cumin powder
2	garlic cloves, minced fine
1 tsp	salt
½ tsp	black pepper

Wear latex gloves while you seed and chop the peppers. Purée all the ingredients in a food processor. The sauce should be about the same consistency as a good mustard. If it is too thick, add more lime juice a little at a time.

Yields approximately ¾ cup

PINEAPPLE
VEAL KABOBS

Veal is more difficult to barbecue because of its low fat content. It can be overcooked very quickly, but it remains tender on kabobs. There's not a lot of work involved in this dish.

2 lbs	veal
1	fresh pineapple
1 cup	orange juice
1/4 cup	olive oil
1 tbsp	onion, grated
1 tbsp	dried whole Mexican oregano

Cut the veal and pineapple into 1 1/2 -inch cubes. Alternate these cubes on skewers to make 16 kabobs. To prevent the pineapple from spinning, use two parallel skewers about 1/2 inch apart.

To prepare a basting sauce, combine the orange juice, oil, onion and oregano in a bowl. Pour the sauce over the skewers in a shallow dish and allow them to stand at room temperature for half an hour or more. Turn the skewers occasionally during this period.

Grill the skewers in a preheated barbecue over a medium heat (350°F) for approximately 20 minutes. Turn them four times so that each side gets grilled only once. Each time you turn the skewers, baste them liberally with the sauce.

Serves 4 to 6

DALMATIAN POLPETA

with tomato and onion relish

1/3 lb lean ground beef
1/3 lb lean ground pork
1/3 lb ground veal
1 large leek
2 medium eggs
2 tbsp black pepper
1 tbsp salt

Polpeta are grilled meat patties. If you prepare the relish and the patties beforehand, you can have dinner on the table in 30 minutes.

Mince the white of the leek very fine. Combine it with the other ingredients in a large bowl. Mix and knead well and shape into 12 round balls. Press the balls into patties, approximately ¾ inch thick. Arrange them on a cookie sheet, cover with food wrap and refrigerate for 6 to 24 hours. This will allow the patties to set. Let the patties come to room temperature before putting them on the barbecue.

Put the polpeta on the grid of a preheated barbecue and grill them over a medium heat (350°F) for 10 minutes a side. Turn the heat to high (400°F) and grill them until they are well browned. Arrange in the centre of a serving platter, surrounded by Tomato and Onion Relish.

Serves 4 to 6

Tomato and onion relish

2 large, dried ancho chilies
3 pieces dried tomato (packed in oil)
3 tbsp olive oil
5 large plum tomatoes, chopped
1 large white onion, chopped
6 garlic cloves, minced
1 tsp sugar
1/2 tsp dried and crushed red chilies

Remove the stems and seeds of the anchos and purée them with the dried tomatoes and 1 tablespoon of olive oil in a food processor. Transfer the purée to a bowl and stir in the tomatoes. Cover with food wrap and set aside, or proceed directly to the next step.

Heat the remaining olive oil in a frying pan. Sauté the onions and garlic until the onions become limp. Stir in the purée, sugar and dried chilies. Simmer until all the liquid has evaporated.

Transfer to a serving bowl. If you make the relish beforehand, heat it before serving.

Yields 1 cup

MONGOLIAN BEEF **RIBS**
WITH **curried peanut sauce**

Butterflying this tough cut of meat and marinating it for 8 to 12 hours will help to soften its texture. The curried peanut sauce finishes off the deed. A butcher will butterfly the ribs for you.

3 lbs	beef short ribs, butterflied
1/2 cup	soy sauce
1/4 cup	olive oil
1/4 cup	dry sherry
1/4 cup	liquid honey
6 tbsp	sesame seeds, toasted
3 tbsp	peanut butter
2 tbsp	curry powder
2 tbsp	black pepper
6	garlic cloves, minced
2 tbsp	green onion, white ends only, minced very fine
1 tbsp	fresh ginger, grated

To prepare a marinade, purée the soy sauce, olive oil, sherry, honey, sesame seeds, peanut butter, curry powder and black pepper in a blender until smooth. Transfer to a bowl and stir in the garlic, green onion and ginger, producing a light paste.

Place the ribs in a glass dish. Pour two-thirds of the marinade over them and reserve the remainder. Cover the ribs with food wrap and refrigerate for 8 to 12 hours.

Dry the ribs with paper towels and put them on the grid of a preheated barbecue. Grill over a low to medium heat (250 to 350°F) for 35 to 40 minutes. Turn and baste with the marinade often. Raise the heat to high (400°F) and grill until the ribs are slightly charred.

Put the reserved marinade in a small saucepan and bring it to a feverish boil. Transfer the ribs to a large serving platter, spoon the hot marinade over top and serve immediately.

Serves 6

PEANUT-SPICED PORK
with fiery DIPPING sauce

2 lbs	very lean pork roast, cut into 1-inch cubes
4 tbsp	peanut butter
2 tbsp	light soy sauce
1 tbsp	cumin powder
2	garlic cloves, minced
1 tbsp	black pepper

These skewers will delight people who crave spicy food. The dipping sauce can be prepared the day before.

Combine the peanut butter, soy sauce, cumin, garlic and pepper in a bowl, producing a paste. Rub this mixture on and into all the pieces of pork. Thread the cubes of pork on skewers. Put them on the grid of a preheated barbecue and grill over a medium heat (350°F). Turn the skewers so that only two opposite sides of the meat get well browned. Continue grilling until these two sides are slightly charred, leaving the inside of the cubes cooked to a medium stage. Serve with Fiery Dipping Sauce.

Serves 4 to 6.

Fiery dipping sauce

¾ cup	dark soy sauce
¼ cup	liquid honey
2	garlic cloves, minced fine
1 tbsp	dried and crushed red chilies
1 tbsp	dry mustard powder
	cold water

Bring the soy sauce, honey, garlic and red chilies to a low simmer in a small saucepan. Combine the mustard powder with just enough water to make a runny paste. Drizzle this into the saucepan and remove from the heat. Ladle into individual dipping bowls and allow to cool to room temperature before serving.

Yields 1 cup

PORK TENDERLOIN with
mustard, lemon and rosemary

Mustard, lemon and rosemary always go well with pork, and the tenderloin is guaranteed to be – what else? – tender. Barbecue-Steamed Yukon Golds with Onions and More Onions (page 152) would make a well-matched side dish.

1	¹⁄₂- to ³⁄₄-lb pork tenderloin
1 tsp	dry mustard powder
¹⁄₄ cup	fresh lemon juice
¹⁄₄ cup	olive oil
1 tbsp	fresh rosemary, minced fine
1	large garlic clove, minced

Rub the entire tenderloin with the dry mustard and place in a shallow glass dish. Combine the remaining ingredients in a bowl. Pour them over the pork, cover and marinate at room temperature for half an hour or more. Turn the tenderloin several times during this period.

Pat the tenderloin dry with paper towels and put it on the grid of a preheated barbecue. Grill over a low to medium heat (250 to 350°F) for approximately 30 minutes. Turn and baste with the marinade often. Do not overcook. The meat should have a slight pink shade to it. Slice every ³⁄₈ inch and serve with your favourite barbecue sauce.

Serves 2

Pork rib revelations

- Baby back ribs usually come from Danish hogs, which are smaller than the North American animal. A rack of 8 or 9 baby back ribs is enough for one person.

- Side ribs are the familiar spareribs. A rack, which weighs about 4 to 5 pounds, will feed 2 people.

- Country style pork ribs are cut from the bottom end of the loin. They have a lot of meat with a bit of bone attached. A 3 ¹⁄₂-pound piece will do for 4 people.

- Ribs are done when you can pinch off a little bit of meat from the bone or when you can easily pull the end bone off a rack.

CHILIED
BABY BACK RIBS

4 racks	baby back ribs, cleaned and trimmed
	meat seasoning spice rub (see page 26)
1 cup	chili sauce
½ cup	water
1	medium onion, grated
2	large garlic cloves, minced
2 tbsp	Worcestershire sauce
2 tbsp	black pepper
1 tbsp	prepared mustard
1 tsp	salt

This requires a little longer cooking time than you may be used to when preparing ribs on a gas barbecue.

Remove the membrane from the bone side of the ribs: slip a paring knife between the bone and the membrane to release it. Work your fingers underneath the membrane until you can grasp it and pull it off the entire length of the rack.

Place the ribs on a cutting board. Sprinkle them liberally with your favourite meat seasoning spice and allow to stand at room temperature for 15 minutes.

Prepare a chili basting sauce by combining the chili sauce, water, onion, garlic, Worcestershire, pepper, mustard and salt in a bowl.

Prepare a gas barbecue for the indirect method of cooking described on page 42. Ignite only one or two burners on a low to medium heat (250 to 350°F).

Arrange the ribs on the unfired area of the grid and barbecue for 1 to 1½ hours at 250 to 300°F. Turn frequently and baste often with the chili sauce mixture.

When the ribs are cooked (you will be able to pull the end bone off easily), move them over to the fired area of the barbecue and grill for a short time until well browned.

Serves 4

rum AND pepper PORK CHOPS
with molasses butter

Firefighters love this one. With the molasses butter prepared the day before, this dish is on the table in less than an hour.

4 centre-cut pork chops, at least ¾ inch thick, bone in, trimmed of fat
⅓ cup dark rum
1 tbsp fresh lime juice
½ tsp salt
4 tbsp coarsely ground black pepper

Combine the rum, lime juice and salt in a bowl. Place the pork chops in a glass dish. Pour the rum mixture over top and allow to sit at room temperature for half an hour or more. Turn the chops often during this time.

Have the pepper in a dish. Pat the chops dry with paper towels and press them into the pepper, coating them evenly.

Put the chops on the grid of a preheated barbecue and grill over a medium heat (350°F) for 15 to 20 minutes, or until done. Turn the chops several times during the cooking period. Top each pork chop with a swirl (½ tbsp) of molasses butter before serving.

Serves 4

Molasses butter

⅛ lb butter, soft
1 tbsp molasses
½ tsp fresh lime juice

Combine the molasses and the soft butter. Beat in the lime juice. Cover and place in the refrigerator overnight (or use immediately).

Yields ¼ cup

BARBECUE
country-style RIBS

3 lbs	country-style pork ribs
¾ cup	orange juice
3 tbsp	olive oil
2 tbsp	fresh lime juice
2	garlic cloves, minced fine
1 tbsp	fresh ginger, grated
1 tsp	dried whole Mexican oregano
½ cup	sweet barbecue sauce

Orange juice and ginger, oregano and sweet barbecue sauce – a fusion recipe of sorts. The ribs marinate for 8 to 24 hours.

Place the ribs in a shallow glass dish.

Prepare a marinade by combining the orange juice, olive oil, lime juice, garlic, ginger and oregano in a bowl. Pour over the ribs, cover and refrigerate for 8 to 24 hours.

Bring the ribs to room temperature and preheat the barbecue. Pat the ribs dry with paper towels and put them on the grid. Grill the ribs over a low to medium heat (250 to 350°F) for 40 to 45 minutes. Turn and baste with the marinade several times.

Raise the heat to high (400°F) and grill for 10 minutes more, or until the ribs become slightly crusted. Turn and baste the ribs with the barbecue sauce often.

Transfer the ribs to a serving platter and sprinkle with salt and pepper before serving.

Serves 4 to 6

CAROLINA'S PORK STEAK

Carolina is a woman
who runs a steak
and chop restaurant
in – you guessed it –
Carolina. She gave
me a list of the ingre-
dients in her pork
steak recipe, and I
experimented until
I got the right
proportions.

4	lean pork steaks, ¾ inch thick
2 tbsp	meat seasoning spice rub (see page 26)
¼ cup	olive oil
3 tbsp	grainy Dijon mustard
3 tbsp	raspberry vinegar
1 tbsp	fresh lime juice
4	large garlic cloves, minced
½ tsp	molasses
½ tsp	dried and crushed red chilies

Trim any outside fat from the steaks. Rub them with your favourite meat seasoning and arrange in a glass dish in one layer.

Prepare a basting sauce by combining the olive oil and mustard in a glass bowl. Add the remaining ingredients and blend them well.

Pour the sauce over the steaks and allow them to sit at room temperature for at least half an hour. Turn the steaks several times during this period.

Pat the steaks dry with paper towels and put them on the grid of a preheated barbecue. Grill over a medium to high heat (350 to 400°F) for approximately 8 minutes a side. Turn and baste with the sauce frequently.

Transfer the steaks to a serving platter and gently season with salt.

Serves 4

SPIT BARBECUE HAM
with orange marmalade glaze

1	14-lb cured, smoked ham
4 tbsp	black pepper
½ cup	olive oil
½ cup	orange marmalade
¼ cup	white wine
1 tbsp	soy sauce
6	garlic cloves, minced fine
2 tbsp	fresh ginger, grated

Remove the rind from the ham, leaving the fat intact and still attached to the meat. Score the fat diagonally, both ways, creating a diamond effect on the surface. Rub the entire ham with the black pepper. Place on the spit rod and barbecue over a medium to high heat (350 to 400°F). Have a drip pan below to catch any drippings and prevent flare-ups.

Prepare a basting sauce by combining the olive oil, marmalade, wine, soy sauce, garlic and ginger in a bowl.

As you barbecue the ham, baste it often with the sauce. Continue to cook for 4 to 5 hours until it is well heated through and the outside becomes browned and crisp.

Serves 10 to 12

Not a quickie. Kick back and enjoy yourself while you let the family take turns basting the meat and checking the cooking temperature.

This ham is usually cooked on a spit over charcoal. On the rotisserie of a gas barbecue, it requires more attention because the spit is closer to the heat.

LEG OF PORK ON THE SPIT

This is basic southern European cookery. Get it on early and enjoy the day, making this a family cookery event. The leg can be done on a gas rotisserie barbecue, but it turns out better on a spit over charcoal, possibly because that's the way it has been done for centuries.

1	12-lb leg of pork, boned, rolled and tied
4 tbsp	black pepper
½ cup	olive oil
½ cup	white wine
¼ cup	soy sauce
6	garlic cloves, minced fine
2 tbsp	fresh ginger, grated

Rub the entire leg with the black pepper. Place the leg on the spit rod and barbecue over medium to high heat (350 to 400°F). Have a pan below to catch the drippings and prevent flare-ups.

Produce a basting sauce by combining the olive oil, white wine, soy sauce, garlic and ginger in a glass bowl. Baste the pork often with the sauce during the entire cooking time.

Cook the leg for 6 hours until it is well done, making sure that the outside becomes well browned and crispy.

Serves 10 to 12

My preference for grilling lamb or doing it on the spit may have something to do with my experience in Texas. Even though I've never liked the taste of barbecued lamb – done in the low and slow method – I decided one year to buy some of our beautiful British Columbia lamb from Saltspring Island and cook it in the competition in Taylor, which is just outside Austin.

I took half a lamb. (It was frozen and in a cooler, which I put in the overhead bin on the plane. I never check my meat with my luggage; I don't care if my clothes arrive, but I can't compete without my meat.) I marinated the lamb and barbecued it on a big charcoal- and wood-burning unit, like my Pitt's and Spitt's. Before submitting the breast and shoulder for judging, I tasted the meat. It was good – the only barbecued lamb that I ever thought tasted good.

GRILLED LAMB AND GAME

I knew it wasn't going to do well, however, because it had a lighter colour, finer texture and milder taste than Texas lamb. In fact, I placed about last in a field of over a hundred. (As a consolation, I barbecued my first goat in that event and took the blue ribbon.)

Pat also had a bad experience in Taylor. She'd entered the wild-game category with cougar meat given to her by a firefighter who had a tag to shoot one that year on his property in the B.C. interior. She did a shoulder roast, rubbed with spice. It came out like a nice, light ham. She labelled it "cougar" and submitted it, but many of the judges refused to taste the samples because they related it to cat.

I still like to eat lamb, but I think people try to dress it up too much. The meat has a delicate flavour that shouldn't be masked. Most of my recipes call for a light marinade and fast grilling – and that produces award-winning lamb, as far as I'm concerned.

Čevapčiči with RED ONION
and sweet MUSTARD

1 ½ lbs   lean ground lamb
1 ½ lbs   ground veal
1   small onion, minced fine
1 tbsp   olive oil
2   garlic cloves, minced very fine
1 tbsp   paprika
2   egg whites, lightly beaten
2   large red onions, thinly sliced

These Croatian grilled sausages are often served as an appetizer on the Adriatic coast. If you make the sausage rolls ahead of time, on the following day you will have a 20-minute dinner preparation.

Heat the oil in a frying pan. Sauté the onion for 10 minutes, stir in the garlic and sauté for an additional 2 minutes. Drain well (this does make a difference) and transfer the onion and garlic to a large bowl. Add the meat, paprika and egg whites to the bowl. Blend the ingredients well. Form into rolls 1 ½ inches in diameter and 4 inches long (like a sausage). Place on a cookie sheet, cover with wax paper and refrigerate for 8 to 24 hours. This will allow the rolls to set.

Leaving a space between them, thread the rolls (lengthwise) on skewers. Two or three will fit on each skewer. Place the skewers on the grid of a preheated barbecue and grill over a high heat (400°F) for approximately 10 minutes, or until well browned. Roll them back and forth across the grid so that all the sides get browned.

Remove the sausages from the skewers, arrange on a bed of red onion slices and serve with Sweet Hot Mustard Sauce.

Serves 4 to 6

Sweet hot mustard sauce

½ cup   brown sugar
¼ cup   mustard powder
1 tbsp   flour
2   eggs, beaten
⅓ cup   water
⅓ cup   fresh lemon juice
2 tbsp   balsamic vinegar

Combine the sugar, mustard powder and flour in a saucepan. Add the beaten eggs and whip with a whisk until smooth. Stir in the water, lemon juice and vinegar and place on a medium heat. Cook and stir until the sauce becomes thick and creamy. Allow to reach room temperature before serving. Keeps well under refrigeration. Yields 1 to 2 cups

SKEWERED
LAMB CHOPS
with MUSHROOMS and TOMATOES

These skewered chops are tops! This marinade has a mid-European taste. The more flavour you desire, the longer you allow the chops to marinate.

8	lean lamb chops
12	small boiling onions
12	large mushroom caps
12	cherry tomatoes
8 oz	canned tomato sauce
½ cup	white wine
¼ cup	fresh lime juice
3 tbsp	olive oil
2 tbsp	hot horseradish
1	medium onion, grated
1 tbsp	Worcestershire sauce
½ tbsp	Mexican oregano powder
½ tsp	rosemary powder
½ tsp	salt

Parboil the onions for 2 minutes. Drain them and place in a bowl along with the mushroom caps and cherry tomatoes. Set aside.

Leaving the bone in, pound out the chops to twice their size and arrange in a shallow glass dish.

Prepare a marinade by blending the remaining ingredients in a food processor until smooth. Pour the marinade over the chops and allow to stand at room temperature for at least half an hour and up to 2 hours.

Remove the meat from the marinade and pat it dry with paper towels. Make 4 kabobs, each with two chops separated by onions, mushroom caps and cherry tomatoes. Thread the chops on the skewers, making two folds in each one. To prevent the vegetables from spinning, use two skewers, parallel and about ¼ to ½ inch apart.

Put the skewers on the grid of a preheated barbecue and grill over a high heat (400°F) for approximately 10 to 15 minutes, until the chops begin to brown well. Turn and baste the chops often with the marinade.

Serves 4

MEDITERRANEAN LAMB
chops with PESTO sauce

8	lean loin lamb chops, 1 inch thick
1/2 cup	olive oil
4	large garlic cloves, chopped
1/4 cup	fresh basil, chopped
1/4 cup	fresh parsley, chopped
2 tbsp	Parmesan cheese, fresh grated
2 tbsp	black pepper
1/2 tsp	salt

Pesto isn't just for pasta. The classic basil, parsley and Parmesan combination makes a marinade that complements lamb chops. An 8- to 24-hour marinating is followed by a quick grilling.

Place the lamb chops in a shallow glass dish in a single layer.

Prepare a pesto sauce by blending the olive oil and garlic in a food processor until the garlic is minced. Add the basil, parsley, cheese, pepper and salt, blending to a smooth creamy mixture. Pour over the lamb chops. Cover with food wrap and refrigerate for 8 to 24 hours.

Remove the chops from the pesto sauce and put them on the grid of a preheated barbecue. Grill over a low to medium heat (250 to 350°F) for 15 minutes. Turn and baste with the pesto sauce several times. Don't cook them beyond a medium stage.

Serves 4 to 6

DIJONED **RACK** OF LAMB

Serve this popular cut of lamb with potatoes, roasted either in the oven or on the barbecue. The marinating period is short and the grilling will take about half an hour.

1	8-rib rack of lamb, trimmed of fat
	salt
¼ cup	grainy Dijon mustard
½ tsp	HP Sauce
3	large garlic cloves, minced
¼ tsp	dried and crushed red chilies

Place the lamb in a shallow glass dish, sprinkle with salt and set aside.

Combine the mustard, HP Sauce, garlic and red chilies in a bowl. Spread this mixture over the entire rack of lamb. Cover with food wrap and hold for half an hour or more.

Put the rack of lamb on the grid of a preheated barbecue and grill over a medium heat (350°F), turning often, until the rack reaches a medium-rare stage, or until an instant thermometer, inserted into the thickest part of the meat, reaches 150 to 160°F.

Arrange on a platter and allow to sit for 5 minutes before serving.

Serves 2

MONTENEGRO'S
LAMB strips

1 lb	loin of lamb, trimmed of fat
4	large roasted red bell peppers (see page 148)
1/4 cup	dried and crushed red chilies
1/3 cup	olive oil
2 tbsp	lime juice
6	large garlic cloves
3 tbsp	cumin powder
1 tbsp	coriander powder
1/2 cup	mayonnaise
2 tbsp	olive oil

Montenegrin restaurants in Croatia have a reputation for serving hotter foods. These lamb strips marinate in the spicy sauce for 6 to 24 hours.

Cut the lamb into strips 1 1/2 inches wide and about 6 inches long. Cut the roasted peppers into wide strips.

To prepare a marinade, purée the red chilies, 1/3 cup olive oil, lime juice, garlic, cumin and coriander in a food processor. Combine the mayonnaise and 2 tbsp olive oil in a glass bowl. Add the purée and blend well.

Add the lamb strips to the bowl and stir to coat all the pieces evenly. Refrigerate for 6 to 24 hours. Stir the meat several times during the marinating period.

Thread the meat in accordion folds onto skewers and place a strip of bell pepper between each piece of meat. To prevent the peppers from spinning, use two skewers parallel and about 1/2 inch apart.

Allow the skewers to sit at room temperature for an hour before putting on the grid of a preheated barbecue. Grill over a medium to high heat (350 to 400°F) until browned, about 5 minutes on each of two sides. Baste with the marinade several times during the cooking period.

Serves 4

SPIT BARBECUE LEG OF
LAMB from the Adriatic

On a spit cooked outdoors over charcoal – this is my favourite way to prepare lamb perhaps because it was always an Easter celebration dinner in my parents' home.

1	5-lb leg of lamb
6	garlic cloves, halved, lengthwise
1 tsp	dried whole Mexican oregano
1/2 tsp	dried and crushed red chilies
1 tsp	salt
1/4 cup	olive oil
1 1/2 tbsp	fresh lime juice

Combine the olive oil and lime juice in a glass bowl and set aside until ready for use.

Make 12 small slits in the lamb and insert a piece of garlic into each one. Rub the entire leg with the oregano, red chilies and salt.

Insert the spit rod almost parallel to the bone. Place it in the rack with a drip pan below to prevent flare-ups.

Barbecue the leg over medium to high heat (350 to 400°F) for 3 to 4 hours. Baste with the olive oil mixture until it is all used and the lamb is well browned on the outside. The meat will done when the internal temperature is 160 to 170°F.

Serves 6 to 8

SPIT-ROASTED
breast of lamb

1	4-lb breast of lamb
3 cups	red wine
1/4 cup	cider vinegar
1/8 cup	fresh lemon juice
4	large garlic cloves, minced very fine
1/2	onion, grated
1 tbsp	fresh basil, minced very fine
1 tbsp	fresh rosemary, minced very fine
1 tbsp	meat seasoning spice rub (any on page 26)
2 tbsp	black pepper

The long marinating will give the lamb a slightly tart and lightly seasoned flavour. The breast is usually cooked on a spit over charcoal, but it can be done on the rotisserie of a gas barbecue if you maintain a watchful eye and a somewhat lower cooking temperature.

Place the breast of lamb in a glass dish.

Prepare a marinade by combining the wine, cider vinegar, lemon juice, garlic, onion, basil and rosemary in a glass bowl. Pour the marinade over the breast and refrigerate for 8 to 24 hours. Turn several times during the marinating period.

Remove the lamb, reserving the marinade. Wipe the breast with paper towels, removing the marinade from the surface. Rub the entire breast with your favourite meat seasoning spice rub and the black pepper.

Weave the breast on the spit rod and place the rod in the rack. Have a drip pan below to prevent flare-ups.

Barbecue the breast over a medium to high heat (350 to 400°F) for 1 to 2 hours until the lamb becomes well browned and crispy. Baste with the reserved marinade regularly during the entire cooking time. The meat will be done when the internal temperature is 160 to 170°F.

Serves 4 to 6

BASICALLY
grilled rabbit

You can purchase fresh farm-grown rabbit at European meat markets, but it can also be found in the frozen foods section at most supermarkets.

1	young farm-grown rabbit, cut into serving pieces
½ cup	olive oil
3 tbsp	fresh lime juice
1 tbsp	celery seed
1 tbsp	black pepper
1	large garlic clove, minced fine
½ tsp	thyme powder
½ tsp	dried whole Mexican oregano
½ tsp	salt

Rinse the rabbit pieces under cold water, pat dry with paper towels and place in a glass dish.

Prepare a basting sauce by blending the remaining ingredients in a food processor. Pour over the rabbit pieces and allow to stand at room temperature for half an hour or more. Turn the pieces occasionally.

Pat dry with paper towels and put the rabbit pieces on the grid of a preheated barbecue. Grill over a medium heat (350°F) for approximately 20 minutes. Turn and baste often with the marinade.

Raise the heat to high (400°F) and grill quickly until the meat is well browned and getting crispy.

Serves 2

Dalmatian Polpeta with Tomato and Onion Relish, p.109

HEAVENLY VENISON chops

8	venison chops, 1 inch thick
1/4 lb	butter, room-temperature soft
2 tbsp	fresh parsley, minced
1 tbsp	mustard powder
1 tbsp	onion, grated
1/4 cup	fresh lime juice
1/4 cup	chili sauce
1 tsp	black pepper
1/2 tsp	salt
1/2 tsp	dried and crushed red chilies

Most recipes for wild game advise marinating to mask the gaminess of the meat. If venison is hunted before the rutting season and cared for properly from the time of the shoot to the time of butchering, it should not have a strong, objectionable flavour.

Beat together the butter, parsley, mustard powder and onion in a small glass bowl. When well blended, shape into a small log and refrigerate until firm.

Prepare a basting sauce by blending together the lime juice, chili sauce, black pepper, salt and red chilies in a glass bowl.

Put the chops on the grid of a preheated barbecue and grill them over a medium heat (350°F) until done to your preference. Rare would take 6 to 12 minutes. Turn the chops only once but baste with the sauce several times during the entire cooking period.

Arrange the chops on a large, heated serving platter. Slice the butter log into 8 equal rounds and place one on top of each chop. Garnish with your favourite fresh herbs.

Serves 4

Mustard-Glazed Chicken Thighs, p. 135

GRILLED POULTRY AND WILDFOWL

The tradition of firefighters cooking at the firehall probably began when they worked twenty-four-hour shifts. Now, while we work ten- and fourteen-hour shifts, we still cook and eat a hot meal together, sharing the cost of the food.

When I'm the cook, I try to buy all the ingredients the day before, usually on my way home from a shift. It's not convenient to shop for groceries while we're working because we can't allow one person to be away from the firehall in case we get a call. If we need to run out to the store, everyone has to suit up, get into the truck and drive to a supermarket. (There's always one near a firehall.) That way we're ready to answer a call. By the way, this practice has never raised our response time.

I suppose we could send out for KFC but why would we do that when barbecuing chicken is quick and easy? Well, the truth is many of my chicken recipes are quick to cook, but they do need a period of marinating—some short, some long. I marinate chicken because you can change its flavour and make it taste like anything you want. Longer periods of marinating create more flavour. Marinades with mustard, because they are so powerful, need a shorter time.

There's one rule with chicken: don't dry it out. You can't make chicken tender by cooking it a long time. You can only cook it to the right moment of doneness—or go too far. There is a fine line between moist and dry, and it's easy to cross.

Heat is a factor in cooking chicken. A low frying heat seems to condemn chicken to rubberiness. Similarly, on the barbecue grill, it's important to have the heat high enough to sear the outside quickly. If the grilling heat is low, by the time the outside is nice and brown, the inside will bounce off your teeth. Chicken can, however, be cooked low and slow in the indirect method of barbecue.

GRILLED CHICKEN

When shopping for poultry look for skin that is white or just off-white and with a sheen. If the skin is drying out and beginning to discolour, don't buy that chicken. Press the flesh lightly with your finger; the meat should feel plump and firm and should return to its original position when released. The fat should be white, firm to the touch and not slimy.

Never thaw frozen poultry in the microwave. You can be guaranteed that some areas will begin to cook and will be overcooked and dry when the rest is just ready.

rosemary AND lime
CHICKEN

2	whole chicken breasts
8	chicken thighs
8	chicken legs
2 cups	olive oil
4 tbsp	fresh lime juice
2 tbsp	dried rosemary, crushed
8	large garlic cloves, coarsely minced
3	bay leaves
1 tsp	white pepper
1 tsp	salt
4	medium vine-ripened tomatoes, cut into wedges
2	large limes, cut into wedges
	fresh rosemary sprigs

This is a Croatian dish my parents used to make. My mother would buy whole chickens, cut them up and put them in the marinade, and the next day my dad would cook them. The chicken can marinate for 8 to 24 hours.

Split the chicken breasts and cut each piece in half crosswise. Arrange the chicken pieces in a large shallow glass dish.

Prepare a marinade by blending the olive oil, lime juice, rosemary, garlic, bay leaves, pepper and salt in a bowl. Pour over the chicken pieces, cover with food wrap and refrigerate for 8 to 24 hours. Turn the chicken pieces several times during this period, making sure that all the pieces are well coated with the marinade.

Pat the chicken pieces dry with paper towels and put them on the grid of a preheated barbecue. Grill them over a medium to high heat (350 to 400°F) for approximately 30 to 45 minutes. Turn and baste with the marinade several times during the cooking period.

Arrange the chicken pieces on a large serving platter. Garnish with the tomato wedges, lime wedges and sprigs of fresh rosemary.

Serves 6

The ALL-CITRUS
chicken

For chicken and pork, I like to use a fruit-juice-based marinade without oil. I enjoy the flavours and the healthful cooking. This chicken marinates for 12 to 24 hours, but the following day dinner will be cooked in 45 minutes.

8	chicken pieces
1 cup	unsweetened pink grapefruit juice
¼ cup	water
¼ cup	fresh lime juice
3 tbsp	brown sugar
1 tsp	dry mustard powder
¼ tsp	nutmeg powder
¼ tsp	salt
1 tbsp	butter
1	small onion, halved and sliced very thin
1 cup	pink grapefruit sections, white membrane removed

Prepare a basting sauce by combining the grapefruit juice, water, lime juice, brown sugar, dry mustard, nutmeg and salt in a small bowl.

Place the chicken pieces in a large glass dish. Pour the grapefruit mixture over them. Cover tightly with food wrap and refrigerate for 12 to 24 hours.

Before grilling, bring the chicken pieces to room temperature. Pat them dry with paper towels and put them on the grid of a preheated barbecue. Grill the chicken over a high heat (400°F) for 10 minutes a side. Lower the heat to medium (350°F). Baste the chicken with the marinade and continue to cook. Turn and baste often with the sauce, cooking until tender and browned on both sides. This will take approximately 30 to 45 minutes.

During the last 5 minutes, melt the butter in a small saucepan and sauté the onions until limp. Stir in the grapefruit sections and keep warm.

Arrange the chicken pieces on a serving platter. Spoon the onion and grapefruit mixture over top and serve immediately.

Serves 4

MUSTARD -GLAZED
chicken thighs

16	chicken thighs
½ cup	sea salt
¼ cup	black pepper
3 tbsp	cumin powder
1 cup	grainy Dijon mustard
¼ cup	prepared mustard
¼ cup	prepared horseradish
¼ cup	white wine
4	large garlic cloves, minced very fine
¾ cup	liquid honey

My mother, the historian in the family, says Germans who came to live on the Croatian coast during the Ottoman Empire introduced mustard into the local cuisine. This is my variation on a German-influenced Croatian dish.

Combine the sea salt, black pepper and cumin in a bowl. Sprinkle the chicken thighs with the spices and place in a glass dish. Cover with food wrap and hold at room temperature for about half an hour.

To prepare a basting sauce, combine the two mustards, horseradish, white wine and garlic in a bowl.

Put the thighs on the grid of a preheated barbecue and grill over a medium to high heat (350 to 400°F). Turn and baste often with the sauce until the skin is crispy. This will take approximately 20 to 30 minutes.

Close the lid of the barbecue and cook on a low to medium heat (250 to 350°F) for another 15 minutes. Baste the meat side of the thighs with the liquid honey and cook for 5 minutes more. The honey will give the thighs a lovely sheen.

Serves 4 to 6

Red currant barbecue
CHICKEN
with a wine shallot sauce

The red currant jelly gives the chicken a refreshing flavour and a beautiful colour, and the shallot sauce adds a creamy finish. Prepare the shallot sauce before you begin to grill the chicken.

8	chicken thighs
3	whole chicken breasts, split
1½ cups	red currant jelly
1 cup	Dijon mustard
2 tbsp	black pepper

Prepare the currant sauce by blending the jelly, mustard and black pepper in a bowl.

Grill the chicken pieces in a preheated barbecue over medium heat (350°F). Turn and baste several times with the red currant sauce for 15 to 20 minutes a side, or until done.

Arrange on a serving platter and top with Wined Shallot Sauce.

Serves 6

Wined shallot sauce

¾ cup	shallots, minced
¾ cup	white wine
¾ cup	white wine vinegar
1 tbsp	balsamic vinegar
1 tsp	black pepper
1 tsp	salt
1 lb	butter

Bring the shallots, wine, vinegars, salt and pepper to a rolling boil in a saucepan until there is only enough liquid left to keep the shallots moist. Whisk in the butter a little at a time, creating a creamy consistency. Spoon over the chicken pieces and serve immediately.

Yields 1½ cups

ORANGE
and herb barbecue CHICKEN

4	small chicken halves
3	garlic cloves
1 tsp	orange zest, freshly grated
1 tsp	salt
½ tsp	rosemary powder
½ tsp	black pepper
½ cup	undiluted frozen orange juice
2 tbsp	cider vinegar
1 tbsp	Worcestershire sauce

Combine the garlic, orange zest, salt, rosemary and black pepper in a bowl.

Do not remove the skin of the chicken halves but release it so that you can spread the garlic mixture between the skin and the flesh.

Prepare a basting sauce by blending the orange juice, vinegar and Worcestershire in a glass bowl.

Barbecue the chicken halves over a medium heat (350°F) until done, approximately 1 hour. Turn and baste with the sauce regularly.

Serves 4

No marinating period for these chicken halves, but an hour on the barbecue, refreshed with an orange-vinegar-Worcestershire basting sauce. Eat this with celery: tie 2 or 3 inner stalks together with butcher's twine and grill for 5 to 8 minutes, basting with olive oil.

BASIC barbecue CHICKEN PIECES with impeccable basting sauce

After the 8-to 24-hour marinating period, this is a quick and basic preparation. Dinner in 40 minutes. The Impeccable Basting Sauce is one I use often on chicken.

2 3-lb chickens, cut into pieces
1/2 cup soy sauce
1/4 cup dry sherry
3 tbsp olive oil
4 garlic cloves, coarsely minced
1 tbsp black pepper
1 tbsp ginger powder
1/2 tsp cumin powder

Place the chicken pieces in a shallow glass dish.

Prepare a marinade by combining the remaining ingredients in a glass jar. Cover with a lid and shake well. Pour over the chicken pieces. Cover with food wrap and refrigerate for 8 to 24 hours. Turn the pieces several times during the marinating period.

Pat the chicken pieces dry with paper towels and put them on the grid of a preheated barbecue. Grill the chicken pieces over a low to medium heat (250 to 350°F) for approximately 40 minutes or until done. Turn and baste often with Impeccable Basting Sauce. Serves 4 to 6

Impeccable basting sauce

1/2 cup ketchup
4 tbsp cider vinegar
1 1/2 tbsp horseradish
3 tbsp brown sugar
1 large garlic clove, minced very fine
1 tsp black pepper
1/2 tsp balsamic vinegar
1/4 tsp thyme powder

Bring the ketchup, cider vinegar, horseradish, brown sugar and garlic to a low simmer in a small saucepan. Simmer for approximately 5 minutes. Remove from the heat and strain through a fine sieve into a glass bowl. Add the black pepper, balsamic vinegar and thyme, blending all the ingredients well.

If you are grilling or oven-roasting chicken, baste with this sauce lightly but often throughout the cooking time. If you are barbecuing chicken (in the low and slow method), baste during the last hour of cooking. Yields approximately 3/4 cup

EL MATADOR
CHICKEN KABOBS

3 lbs	chicken breasts, skinless and boneless
1 cup	Melinda's XXXtra Hot Sauce (or your favourite)
1 cup	sesame seeds
1/2 cup	soy sauce
1/4 cup	water
1/4 cup	fresh lime juice
1	Granny Smith apple, chopped
1	garlic clove, chopped
2 tbsp	white sugar
1/4 cup	Melinda's XXXtra Hot Sauce
14 oz	canned water chestnuts
16	shiitake mushrooms, quartered

Half an hour in the hot hot sauce, 10 minutes on the hot hot grill and, olé, we've fused Spain, Japan and North America. Cool the palate with potatoes baked on the barbecue, corn on the cob and a plain green salad.

Cut the chicken breasts into 1-inch cubes and place the cubes and the cup of hot sauce in a glass bowl. Cover with food wrap and refrigerate for half an hour. Turn the breasts several times during this period.

To prepare a basting sauce, sauté the sesame seeds over a medium heat in a frying pan until they are lightly browned. Transfer them to a food processor. Add the soy sauce, water, lime juice, apple, garlic, sugar and the 1/4 cup hot sauce. Process until puréed. Transfer the basting sauce to a bowl.

Remove the chicken pieces from the hot sauce and discard the sauce. Starting and ending with 2 chicken pieces, alternate chicken cubes, water chestnuts and mushrooms on skewers to make 12 kabobs. To prevent the vegetables from spinning, use two parallel skewers about 1/4 to 1/2 inch apart.

Grill the kabobs over medium heat (350°F) until done, approximately 10 to 12 minutes. Turn and baste often with some of the sesame sauce.

Bring the remaining sesame sauce to a boil. Put it in individual dipping bowls and serve along with the chicken. Serves 6

Citrus and spice
DRUMETTES

Everyone loves drumettes. These have a southwestern spice in an Asian peanut butter sauce. The vegetables go on the barbecue at the same time as the chicken.

40	large drumettes, skin removed
1/4 cup	fresh lime juice
4 tbsp	soy sauce
4 tbsp	brown sugar
2 tbsp	cumin powder
1 lb	fresh string beans, cleaned and tipped
1	large red bell pepper, halved and seeded
1	large yellow bell pepper, halved and seeded
1/2 cup	olive oil
1/4 cup	chunky peanut butter
1	medium white onion, minced fine
4 tbsp	Melinda's XXXtra Hot Sauce (or your favourite)
3 tbsp	liquid honey
2 tbsp	fresh lime juice
1 tbsp	fresh cilantro, minced fine

Prepare a basting sauce by combining the 1/4 cup lime juice, soy sauce, sugar and cumin in a small bowl.

In a small saucepan, whisk together the olive oil, peanut butter, white onion, hot sauce, honey, 2 tbsp lime juice and the fresh cilantro. Have the saucepan on the stove ready to heat to a simmer when the chicken is cooked.

Tie the string beans together in bunches of 6 to 8. Brush the string beans and peppers with some oil. Place the vegetables and the drumettes on the grid of a preheated barbecue over a medium to high heat (350 to 400°F). When the vegetables begin to char, remove them to a plastic bag, seal tightly and set aside.

Continue to grill the drumettes until they become crispy, and then begin to baste with the sauce. Turn and baste often for about 10 minutes until they are done. Arrange the drumettes in the centre of a large serving platter.

Remove the vegetables from the plastic bag to a cutting board and coarsely chop them. Distribute them on the serving platter around the chicken.

Bring the peanut butter sauce to a simmer and pour it over the chicken and vegetables. Serves 4 to 6

CHICKEN
breast vinaigrette

2	large fresh artichokes
4	small chicken breasts, boned and skinned
2	large red bell peppers, halved and seeded
1	green bell pepper, halved and seeded
2	red onions, halved
8 oz	marinated artichoke hearts, drained and chopped
1/2 cup	pitted black olives, drained and halved
1/2 cup	olive oil
1/4 cup	red wine vinegar
2 tbsp	onion, minced fine
2	large garlic cloves, minced very fine
1/2 tbsp	fresh basil, minced fine
1/2 tbsp	capers, drained
1/2 tbsp	black pepper
1/2 tbsp	balsamic vinegar
1/2 tbsp	salt

Here's another one for the firehall because it will hold until we're back from a call. When the family can't all eat dinner at the same time, you can serve it to some at room temperature or to latecomers chilled.

Cut off the stems of the fresh artichokes. Trim off about a quarter of the top leaves and snap off any tough bottom leaves. Steam for 45 minutes until tender.

Put the chicken breasts on the grid of a preheated barbecue and grill over a medium to high heat (350 to 400°F) for 5 to 7 minutes a side. When the juices run clear, remove them from the barbecue, cover with food wrap and allow to cool.

While the chicken cools, run toothpicks through the onion halves (to hold them together). Grill them and the bell peppers until they begin to char. Place in a plastic bag, seal tightly and set aside for 10 minutes. Remove the vegetables from the bag and allow them to cool.

Slice the chicken and the vegetables into 1/4-inch strips and combine the chicken, vegetables, artichoke hearts and olives in a large serving bowl and toss gently.

Whisk together the remaining ingredients and drizzle over the salad. Toss gently and place on individual salad plates. Garnish with the steamed artichokes cut into pieces. Serves 4 to 6

BALSAMIC TURKEY STEAKS

Sliced turkey breasts grill perfectly. The overnight marinating enhances the flavour and the basting sauce is a must.

1	entire turkey breast, frozen
1 cup	olive oil
2 tbsp	balsamic vinegar
1/2 cup	butter
1/4 cup	white wine
1 tbsp	fresh lime juice
1 tbsp	black pepper
1/2 tsp	salt

Have your butcher slice the frozen breast on a band saw into 1-inch transverse slices, starting at the front of the breastbone and cutting back to where the thighs would join. One slice should be enough for 2 servings. Keep any remaining turkey frozen for later use.

Put 4 frozen slices of turkey in a shallow glass dish. Blend together the olive oil and balsamic vinegar. Pour over the turkey steaks and refrigerate for 8 to 24 hours. Turn the steaks several times during the defrosting period. Discard the marinade and allow the steaks to reach room temperature.

Prepare a basting sauce by melting the butter in a small saucepan, stir in the wine, lime juice, pepper and salt and remove from the heat.

Pat the steaks dry with paper towels and place on the grid of a preheated barbecue. Grill the steaks over a medium to high heat (350 to 400°F) for 6 to 8 minutes a side. Turn the steaks several times and baste often with the sauce.

When cooked the 4 steaks will come apart easily at the breast bone and divide into 8 portions.

Bring any remaining sauce to a boil. Spoon a little sauce over each serving.

Serves 4 to 6

Turkey **KABOBS**

with corn, zucchini and peppers

1   ½-lb turkey tenderloin
½ cup   olive oil/vinegar salad dressing
4   cobs of corn
2   zucchini, cut into 1-inch lengths
2   red bell peppers, seeded
¼ cup   olive oil
2 tbsp   black pepper
1 tbsp   fresh lime juice

These tangy skewers will bring your family running to the dinner table. After you marinate the turkey overnight, the grilling on the barbecue takes only 20 minutes, time enough to cook potatoes or rice.

Cut the turkey into 1-inch cubes and place the cubes and salad dressing in a plastic bag that zips closed. Seal and refrigerate overnight.

Parboil the corn for about 4 to 6 minutes. Put the cobs in cold water to stop the cooking process. Cut each cob into 3 2-inch lengths. Cut the zucchini into 1-inch lengths and the peppers into 1-inch squares.

Discard the salad dressing and drain the turkey pieces. Alternate the turkey cubes, corn, zucchini and red bell peppers on skewers to make about 10 kabobs. To prevent the vegetables from spinning, use two parallel skewers ¼ to ½ inch apart.

Combine the olive oil, black pepper and lime juice in a bowl.

Grill the kabobs in a preheated barbecue over a low to medium high heat (250 to 350°F) for 15 to 20 minutes. Turn and baste often with the olive oil mixture.

Serves 4

Grilled DUCKLING
with PUMPKIN SEEDS

Winter is a good time to serve duckling. Supermarkets seem to have more fresh ducks in that season. Duckling works well on the barbecue because of its fat content.

2	ducklings, quartered
1/4 cup	water
1/2 cup	sweet sherry
1/3 cup	liquid honey
2 tbsp	soy sauce
1 tsp	fresh ginger, grated
1 tsp	mustard powder
1/4 cup	salted pumpkin seeds, lightly toasted

Leaving the skin on the duckling, trim off as much excess fat as possible and place the pieces in a shallow dish.

Prepare a basting sauce by combining the sherry, honey, soy sauce, ginger and mustard powder in a bowl. Bring the water to a low simmer in a saucepan and stir in the sherry-honey mixture. Simmer briefly but do not boil.

Pour the sauce over the duckling pieces and set aside for 15 minutes. Turn the pieces several times during this period.

Pat the duckling pieces dry with paper towels and put them on the grid of a preheated barbecue. Grill the duckling over a medium to high heat (350 to 400°F) until well browned, approximately 10 to 15 minutes a side. Turn and baste often with the marinade during the grilling period.

Arrange on a serving platter and sprinkle with the toasted pumpkin seeds and serve.

Serves 4

ULTRA grilled
DUCK BREAST with hot peanut sauce

4	duck breasts, boned
½ cup	soy sauce
2 tbsp	olive oil
2 tbsp	balsamic vinegar
4	large garlic cloves, minced fine
1 tbsp	molasses
1 tbsp	fresh ginger, grated

After a short marinating and a quick grilling, the breasts are sliced and served with a sauce that will surely raise your temperature.

Place the duck breasts, skin side down, in a shallow glass dish.

Prepare a basting sauce by combining the remaining ingredients and pouring it over the breasts. Allow to stand at room temperature for at least half an hour. Turn the breasts once during the marinating period.

Pat the breasts dry with paper towels and put them, skin side down, on the grid of a preheated barbecue and grill over medium to high heat (350 to 400°F) for approximately 8 minutes. Baste the breasts often. Turn and grill for 8 minutes more, continuing to baste often.

Slice the breasts crosswise on the bias at half-inch intervals. Serve immediately with Peanut Sauce.

Serves 4 to 6

Peanut sauce

½ cup	smooth peanut butter
3 tbsp	white onion, grated
3 tbsp	sweet hot sauce (e.g., Tiger Sauce)
2 tbsp	black pepper
2 tbsp	soy sauce
2	garlic cloves, minced very fine
2 tbsp	2 per cent milk
1 tsp	molasses

Blend all the ingredients in a glass bowl until smooth. Place the sauce in the centre of the platter, surrounded by the sliced duck breasts.

Yields ½ cup

GRILLED VEGETABLES

GRILLED VEGETABLES

Most vegetables are grilled rather than barbecued. They should be done over a medium to high heat. Baste them with oil or butter and turn occasionally. Try not to overcook vegetables; choose ones that will cook in approximately the same time as your main course. The grilling times for vegetables do not vary a great deal. With a little practice, you will be able to coordinate any vegetable cooking with the main course.

The most successful way to hold vegetables, if they are done too soon, is to wrap them in food wrap. Return them to the barbecue for two to three minutes on a high heat before serving.

The grilling times below are estimates. Cook your vegetables until they reach the tenderness and texture that you prefer.

Roasting Red Bell Peppers on the Barbecue

Red bell peppers are the most widely used in roasting. Cut the stem out with a sharp knife. Using a teaspoon, scrape out as many seeds as you can. Wash the peppers well to remove any remaining seeds, set aside and allow to dry.

Place the peppers on the barbecue over a high heat (400°F). Grill, turning often, until they are charred on all sides. This will take 5 to 8 minutes. Remove the peppers and place them in a plastic bag that can be zipped shut.

After 10 minutes, take the peppers from the bag and allow them to cool. Peel off the charred skin over a bowl so you can collect all the oil and juices.

The peppers could be returned to the barbecue to heat before serving or kept for later use. To store, put the peeled peppers and their juices in a glass jar and cover with olive oil. Place a tight-fitting lid on the jar and store in the refrigerator for 3 to 5 weeks.

Vegetable Grilling Tips

Baste vegetables with oil or melted butter as they cook.

ASPARAGUS: Tie 6 to 8 stalks together with cotton twine (butcher's twine) and grill for 8 to 10 minutes.

BELL PEPPERS: Cut peppers in half lengthwise. Remove the stems, seeds and white membranes. Grill 10 to 15 minutes. Barbecue in indirect heat for 30 to 40 minutes.

CORN ON THE COB: Pull back the husks, leaving them attached. Remove the silk, fold the husks back around the corn. Soak in cold water for 10 minutes. Barbecue on the unfired side of the grid for 20 to 30 minutes.

EGGPLANT: Slice into ½-inch to ¾-inch slices. Grill for 10 minutes.

GARLIC: Slice off enough of the top of the garlic head to expose all the cloves. Place on a piece of aluminum foil and sprinkle with paprika. Pour ¼ tsp of olive oil over the exposed cloves. Wrap tightly in the foil and barbecue over a medium heat on the unfired side of the grid for 25 to 35 minutes.

LEEKS: Grill whole for 8 to 15 minutes or barbecue on the unfired side of the grid for 45 to 60 minutes. Grill halved leeks for 3 to 10 minutes until the cut side is lightly charred.

MUSHROOMS: Use whole mushrooms, 1½ inches to 2 inches in diameter. Grill for 10 to 12 minutes.

ONIONS: Leave the skin on whole onions and grill over medium to high heat until the outside is charred and the onion begins to get supple. Grill quartered onions about 10 to 15 minutes until lightly charred. Half-inch thick slices: grill until tender, about 5 to 8 minutes.

POTATOES: Use potatoes no larger than 2 inches in diameter. Parboil them in their skins for 15 minutes. Drain and place in cold water. Grill whole for 15 to 20 minutes. Yukon golds are by far the best for grilling. My second choice would be new white or red potatoes.

TOMATOES: Grill whole until they begin to char, turning often. Place halves on the grid, cut side up, and grill for 6 to 8 minutes. Grill ½-inch to ¾-inch slices for 2 to 5 minutes.

ZUCCHINI: Cut in half lengthwise. Grill for 8 to 15 minutes.

Barbecue CORN
WITH BUTTERED CHEESE

A mid- to late-summer favourite. I use the super-sweet or peaches-and-cream varieties.

8 ears fresh corn
1/4 lb butter
1 tbsp Parmesan cheese, fresh grated
1 tsp black pepper
        salt

Carefully pull the husks back and remove the silk. Using a damp paper towel, brush downward on the cobs to remove any remaining silk. Replace the husks and soak the cobs in very cold water for 10 minutes.

Grill over a medium heat (350°F) for 15 minutes, turning the cobs often.

Melt the butter in a small saucepan, remove from the heat and stir in the black pepper and cheese.

Remove the husks, sprinkle the cobs with salt and serve with the melted butter mixture.

Serves 4 to 6

Hot CORN on the COB

4 ears	fresh corn
1/4 cup	butter
2 tbsp	olive oil
1 tbsp	paprika powder
1 tsp	dried and crushed red chilies
1/2 tsp	salt
1/4 tsp	black pepper

This is the way my relatives love their corn, with a spicy basting sauce setting off the sweetness of the chewier-than-usual kernels.

Remove and discard the husks and all the silk.

Combine the remaining ingredients in a small saucepan until the butter has melted and they are well blended.

Grill the corn over a medium to high heat (350 to 450°F) for 20 to 30 minutes, or until the corn begins to turn a golden brown colour. Turn and baste with the butter mixture frequently.

Serves 2 to 4

Barbecue-steamed
YUKON GOLDS

These yellow-fleshed potatoes remain firm and so tasty when steamed on the barbecue.

6	medium Yukon gold potatoes
3	small onions
1 bunch	green onions, chopped
1 tsp	paprika
1 tsp	black pepper
1/2 tsp	salt
1/4 lb	butter

Peel and quarter the potatoes and the onions.

Cut a piece of aluminum foil large enough to hold all the vegetables when it has been folded in half. Carefully place the vegetables in the centre of the doubled piece of foil and sprinkle them with the spices. Cut the butter into pieces and distribute over top of the vegetables.

Fold and seal the aluminum foil tightly around the vegetables. Place the packet on the barbecue over a medium heat (350°F). Steam for 30 to 45 minutes.

Serves 4 to 6

with onions and more onions

GRILLED CRISPY
POTATOES

8	medium red potatoes
4 tbsp	olive oil
2 tbsp	butter
1/4 cup	fresh parsley, minced
2 tbsp	green onion, minced very fine
1 tbsp	black pepper

Parboiling the potatoes will help them cook more evenly on the barbecue.

Leaving the potatoes unpeeled, put them in water in a saucepan. Bring the water to a boil, shut off the heat and allow the potatoes to sit in the hot water.

Heat the olive oil in a small saucepan. Stir in the butter, parsley, green onion and black pepper and remove from the heat.

Drain the potatoes and allow to cool. Peel and halve them, and place on the barbecue over a medium to high heat (350 to 400°F). Turn and baste with the olive oil mixture frequently, until the potatoes are well browned.

Serves 4 to 6

HEAVENLY POLENTA
slices with sour cream and garlic

A staple in Croatian households, polenta is time-consuming to prepare, but it can be made as much as three days ahead, with the final grilling taking only 10 minutes.

1 cup	yellow cornmeal
4 cups	cold water
2 tsp	salt
2 tbsp	butter
3 tbsp	sour cream
¼ cup	olive oil
4	large garlic cloves, minced fine
3 tbsp	fresh parsley, minced
1 tbsp	black pepper

Bring the water and salt to a boil in a medium saucepan. Stir in the cornmeal a little at a time. Stir constantly and simmer over a medium heat until the cornmeal thickens. This will take about 20 to 25 minutes. At this point the polenta will release from the sides of the pot. When the polenta is fairly firm, stir in the butter and sour cream. Blend well and cook for 5 minutes more.

Pour the polenta onto a platter or an unmarred plastic cutting board. (I keep one just for this purpose.) Shape into a circle approximately 3 inches thick. Cover with food wrap and refrigerate.

When you are ready to cook, slice the polenta into ¾-inch thick slices – 8 should be enough for 4 people. (You will have leftover polenta, which will keep for several days in the refrigerator.) Combine the olive oil, garlic, parsley and black pepper in a bowl. Grill the polenta in a preheated barbecue over a medium to high heat (350 to 400°F), turning and basting the slices with the oil mixture, until grill marks appear on the surface and all the basting sauce is used, about 3 minutes a side. Serve with Barbecue Garlic Paste (see page 33).

Serves 4 or more

Yukons and GARLIC

6	medium Yukon gold potatoes
1 tsp	black pepper
1 tsp	coarse sea salt
½ cup	olive oil
4	large garlic cloves, minced
1 tsp	fresh cilantro, minced very fine

Here are those luscious yellow-fleshed potatoes again, but this time combined with garlic.

Leaving the skins on, parboil the potatoes. Allow to cool and then slice in half. Sprinkle the cut edges with the pepper and salt. With the flat of a wide-bladed knife, press the pepper and salt into the potatoes.

Combine the olive oil, garlic and cilantro in a bowl.

Grill the potatoes over a medium heat (350°F) until the cut side becomes crispy. Turn the halves over and baste frequently with the olive oil mixture, grilling for 20 minutes more.

Serves 4

TOMATOES

STUFFED with CHEESE, PARSLEY and CILANTRO

The tomatoes can be stuffed the night before and stored in the refrigerator.

6	medium tomatoes
6 tbsp	fine bread crumbs
6 tbsp	feta cheese, crumbled
3 tbsp	fresh parsley, minced
1 tbsp	fresh cilantro, minced very fine
1 tbsp	black pepper
1/4 tsp	salt
1/8 tsp	garlic, minced very fine

Cut a thin slice from the stem end of the tomatoes, just large enough to remove the pulp. Place the pulp in a small bowl and put the tomato cups aside.

Strain out the seeds and chop the pulp. Blend in 2 tbsp of the cheese and the remaining ingredients. Fill the tomato cups with this mixture and spoon the remaining cheese equally over top.

Grill the tomatoes over low to medium heat (250 to 350°F) for 5 minutes. Cover lightly with a piece of aluminum foil and grill for 10 minutes more.

Serves 4

BELL PEPPER
salad with mushrooms and ancho chilies

2	large red bell peppers
1	large yellow bell pepper
1	green bell pepper
10	large mushrooms, quartered
1	dried ancho chili pepper
5 tbsp	olive oil
2 tbsp	balsamic vinegar
1 tbsp	vinegar
1 tbsp	fresh lime juice
1 tbsp	black pepper
½ tsp	sea salt

A hot salad with a lightly smoked ancho chili pepper. Serve as a salad or as a main course for vegetarians.

Soften the ancho chili pepper in hot water, seed it and mince very fine. Remove the stems, seeds and white membrane from all the bell peppers. Slice them lengthwise into ½-inch strips and set aside with the quartered mushrooms.

Prepare a dressing by combining the remaining ingredients in a glass bowl.

Place the vegetables on the barbecue using a grill grid that prevents smaller items from falling into the fire. Grill over a medium heat (350°F) until the mushrooms are heated and the peppers have a slightly charred look.

Transfer the vegetables to a shallow salad bowl. Drizzle the dressing over top and toss to coat the vegetables.

Serves 4

RASPBERRY VINAIGRETTE
SALAD

with onion, endive, mushroom and tomato

Buy Walla Wallas as soon as you see them because the season is short. The fruity flavour of the raspberry vinegar shines through.

1	Walla Walla onion
2	large Belgium endives
8	large shiitake mushrooms
8	cherry tomatoes
	olive oil
½ cup	olive oil
¼ cup	fresh lime juice
1 tbsp	raspberry vinegar
½ tbsp	balsamic vinegar
1 tsp	black pepper
½ tsp	sugar
1 cup	arugula, coarsely chopped

Skin, trim and quarter the onions. Stick a toothpick through the centre of each onion quarter to hold them together and grill over a medium to high heat (350 to 400°F) for 5 to 8 minutes, turning them often.

Wash and trim the Belgium endives and cut them in half. Add the endives, mushrooms and tomatoes to the barbecue and grill for 10 to 15 minutes. Turn all the vegetables often and baste with olive oil during the entire grilling time. The onions and endives should be lightly charred before all the vegetables are removed from the barbecue. Hold the vegetables in a large bowl.

Prepare a dressing by blending the ½ cup olive oil, lime juice, raspberry vinegar, balsamic vinegar, black pepper and sugar in a food processor.

Arrange ¼ cup of arugula on each salad plate. Distribute equal amounts of the salad ingredients over the arugula, drizzle the dressing over top and serve.

Serves 4

ZESTY VEGETABLES
with a lime balsamic sauce

6	small leeks
4	large plum tomatoes
2	red onions
1	small eggplant
8	large shiitake mushrooms
2	yellow peppers
2	medium zucchini
4 cups	cold water
5 tbsp	sea salt
6 tbsp	olive oil
4 tbsp	fresh lime juice
1 tsp	lime zest, fresh grated
6	large garlic cloves, minced coarse
½ tbsp	balsamic vinegar
2 tbsp	fresh parsley, minced
1 tbsp	black pepper

A vegetarian or non-vegetarian delight. The marinating in sea salt really brings out the flavours of all the vegetables. With just some rice or baguette bread, this could be a meal in itself.

Trim the leeks, cut them in half lengthwise and carefully wash them. Cut the tomatoes in half. Skin and quarter the onions and run a toothpick through the quarters to hold them together. Peel and slice the eggplant in ¾-inch rings. Remove the stems of the mushrooms. Quarter and seed the peppers. Cut the zucchini in half lengthwise.

Place all the vegetables except the tomatoes in a large bowl. Stir the water and salt together in another bowl and then pour over the vegetables. Make sure all the vegetables are covered and refrigerate for at least 1 hour.

Prepare a basting sauce by blending the remaining ingredients in a glass jar. Allow to stand at room temperature while the vegetables are in the brine. Shake the jar several times during this period.

Drain the vegetables and pat them dry. Using a grill topper, arrange all the vegetables in the barbecue. The tomatoes should be placed with the cut side up and not turned. The other vegetables should be carefully turned several times.

Grill over a medium to high heat (350 to 400°F), basting several times. All the vegetables will be ready within 9 to 15 minutes. Serves 6

A HOT MEXICAN FIESTA of vegetables

This matches up well with fajitas.

12	small red new potatoes
12	small plum tomatoes
3	medium sweet onions
12	large green onions
1 bunch	young asparagus
6	sweet Anaheim red peppers
	butcher's twine
½ cup	olive oil
¼ cup	fresh lime juice
4	garlic cloves, minced
1 tbsp	black pepper
1 tbsp	dried and crushed red chilies
1 tsp	cumin powder
¼ tsp	mustard powder

Boil the potatoes for 10 minutes. Drain and place in very cold water and allow to stand for 10 minutes. Cut 4 very small slits in each tomato. Clean the green onions and cut a small slit in the white end of each one.

Alternate the potatoes, tomatoes and sweet onions on skewers. To prevent the vegetables from spinning, use two skewers, parallel and ¼ to ½ inch apart. With butcher's twine, tie the green onions and asparagus into 4 bunches of each.

Prepare a basting sauce by blending the olive oil, lime juice, garlic, pepper, chilies, cumin and mustard in a food processor on a high speed for 1 minute.

Grill the skewers over a medium to high heat (350 to 400°F) for 10 to 12 minutes, turning them often. Remove and set aside.

Grill the bunches of green onions and asparagus and the sweet red peppers for 10 minutes. Turn and baste often with the sauce. Raise the heat to high and return the potato skewers to the barbecue. Cook all the vegetables until they just begin to char, turning and basting often with the sauce.

Serves 4 to 6

Grilled VEGETABLES
with PEANUT SAUCE

4	medium zucchini, cut into 1-inch pieces
14 oz	canned baby corn, drained
1 lb	large mushrooms
12	cherry tomatoes
1/4 cup	olive oil
1 tsp	fresh lime juice

East meets West in a peanut-sauce slather.

Cut 3 or 4 tiny knife-point slits in each cherry tomato. Place all the vegetables in a glass bowl. Prepare a marinade by combining the olive oil and lime juice. Pour over the vegetables and allow to stand at room temperature for half an hour. Stir gently several times.

Pat the vegetables dry with paper towels and alternate them on four skewers. To prevent them from spinning, use two parallel skewers about 1/4 to 1/2 inch apart.

Grill over a medium to high heat (350 to 400°F) for 6 to 8 minutes. Turn and baste them with the marinade often.

Serves 4

Peanut sauce

4 tbsp	olive oil
1 1/2 cups	mushrooms, chopped
1 bunch	green onions, chopped
3/4 cup	salted peanuts
1/2 cup	water
1/4 cup	sweet hot sauce (e.g., Tiger Sauce)
2 tbsp	soy sauce
1 tsp	black pepper

Heat the olive oil in a saucepan. Sauté the mushrooms for 5 minutes. Add the green onion and sauté for 5 minutes more. Transfer the mushrooms and onions to a blender or food processor. Add the peanuts and water. Blend until the sauce reaches a smooth consistency.

Return the sauce to the saucepan and add the hot sauce, soy sauce and pepper. Bring the sauce to a boil. Lower the heat and simmer for 5 minutes. Place in a gravy boat and serve with the grilled vegetables. Yields 3/4 cup

PIQUANT PINEAPPLE SLICES

Quick, easy and refreshing. Serve with pork or chicken.

1	medium pineapple, peeled and cored
2 tbsp	fresh lime juice
1 tbsp	olive oil
1 tbsp	lime zest, fresh grated
½ tbsp	balsamic vinegar
1 tsp	black pepper

Slice the pineapple crosswise into ¾-inch-thick slices. Combine the olive oil, lime juice and zest, vinegar and pepper in a glass bowl and mix well. Grill the pineapple over a medium to high heat (350 to 400°F) turning and basting frequently with the olive oil mixture until lightly browned and softened. This will take approximately 8 to 12 minutes.

Serves 6

SPANISH VEGGIE BURGER

2	large leeks, chopped
2 tbsp	olive oil
1	large garlic clove, minced very fine
¾ lb	wild or shiitake mushrooms, chopped
2	large plum tomatoes, peeled, seeded and chopped
2	red bell peppers
½ lb	fresh spinach, coarsely chopped
1 tbsp	black pepper
¼ tsp	thyme powder
⅛ tsp	dried and crushed red chilies
½ cup	fine bread crumbs
¼ cup	Parmesan cheese, freshly grated
3	large eggs
4 slices	provolone cheese, large enough to cover the patties
8 slices	French bread, 1 inch thick and lightly toasted
2 tbsp	Barbecue Garlic Paste (see page 33)
	butter
	alfalfa sprouts

This is my special blend of vegetables, spices and herbs to create the perfect vegetarian burger pattie. You can prepare extra patties because they keep well when frozen.

Roast and peel the red peppers (see page 148). Slice them lengthwise.

Heat the olive oil in a frying pan, add the leeks and sauté until limp. Stir in the garlic, mushrooms, tomato, roasted bell peppers, spinach, black pepper, thyme and red chilies. Sauté for 5 to 8 minutes more, drain and place in a bowl.

Gently blend in the bread crumbs and grated cheese, add the eggs and mix well. Form into four equal patties, place on a cookie sheet, cover with food wrap and refrigerate for 4 to 8 hours.

Grill the patties over a medium heat (350°F) for 3 minutes. Turn and place a slice of cheese on each pattie and grill until the cheese is melted. Cook the patties only long enough to heat them through the centre.

Spread the Barbecue Garlic Paste on 4 slices of the lightly toasted bread, place a pattie on top and finish with the alfalfa sprouts. Butter the other slices of the toasted bread and put on top of the burger.

Serves 4

BUTTERED
portabellas

For grilling, these are the elite of mush-rooms. They can be served with a main course or as an appetizer.

2	large portabella mushrooms
¾ cup	butter, melted
½ cup	olive oil
6	large garlic cloves, minced very fine
½ tsp	black pepper
¼ tsp	salt
½	lime
¼ cup	fresh parsley, minced
1	small loaf baguette bread

Prepare a dressing by heating the butter and ¼ cup of the olive oil in a saucepan. Add the garlic, black pepper and salt. Sauté for 5 to 8 minutes, making sure not to brown the garlic.

Cut the bread into ¾-inch slices and grill the slices with the mushrooms over a medium to high heat (350 to 400°F), brushing lightly and frequently with the remaining ¼ cup of olive oil. When the baguette is toasted, remove and place in a bread basket. Grill the mushrooms until they are heated through and beginning to brown slightly. Remove them to a cutting board, slice thinly and place in a shallow serving bowl.

Heat the dressing, drizzle over the portabellas and toss lightly. Squeeze the lime juice over the top, sprinkle with parsley and serve immediately with the grilled baguette bread.

Serves 4

GRILLED DESSERTS

Rummed-up
NECTARINES

Make sure the nectarines you purchase are ripe but still firm. If you do not care to use alcohol when cooking, replace the rum with half molasses and half maple syrup.

6	large firm nectarines
$^{1}/_{4}$ cup	dark rum
$^{1}/_{4}$ cup	liquid honey
1 tbsp	black pepper

Skin, pit and cut the nectarines in half. Place them on a cutting board with the cut side facing up.

Prepare a basting sauce by blending the remaining ingredients in a bowl. Baste the cut side of the nectarines with the sauce.

Put the nectarines on the barbecue, cut side down and grill over a high heat (400°F) until lightly browned.

Baste with the sauce, turn them over and again baste the cut side. Grill for 2 to 3 minutes more. Remove from the barbecue and arrange in a shallow serving dish.

Warm any leftover basting sauce, drizzle over the nectarines and serve immediately.

Serves 4 to 6

NECTARINES WITH
RASPBERRY
sauce

4	large nectarines
1/4 cup	raspberry vinegar
1/4 cup	water
1/2 cup	brown sugar
1/4 tsp	lime zest, fresh grated
1/8 tsp	vanilla extract

A fine dessert, but also a side dish for grilled chicken and pork.

Prepare a basting sauce by bringing the vinegar and water to a low simmer in a small saucepan. Stir in the brown sugar and simmer until the sugar is dissolved. Remove from the heat and stir in the lime zest and vanilla.

Cut the nectarines in half. Pit and peel them. Put them in a glass dish. Ladle the sauce over the nectarines and refrigerate overnight. Turn the nectarines several times during the marinating time.

Remove the nectarines and set aside. Return the sauce to a saucepan and simmer until it is reduced by half.

Place the nectarines, cut side down, on the barbecue, over a medium to high heat (350 to 400°F). Grill and baste with the sauce until lightly browned. Carefully turn with a pair of tongs and grill for an additional minute or so.

Arrange the nectarines in a serving dish. Spoon the remaining sauce into the pit holes and serve.

Serves 4

Balsamic grilled
FRUITS

The mellow tartness of the balsamic vinegar blends well with the sweetness of the three fruits.

½	cantaloupe
½	honeydew melon
1	pineapple
½ cup	butter, melted
¾ cup	port
¾ cup	brown sugar
½ cup	balsamic vinegar
1 tbsp	black pepper
½ tbsp	fresh mint, minced fine

Cut the cantaloupe and melon into wedges, remove the seeds and pare off the skin. Peel the pineapple, remove the core and cut the fruit into spears from top to bottom.

Grill the fruit over a medium to high heat (350 to 400°F) for 6 to 8 minutes. Baste frequently with the melted butter. Arrange on a large serving platter in a single layer.

Bring the port and brown sugar to a boil in a saucepan. Lower the heat and simmer, stirring often until the mixture is reduced by half. Stir in the vinegar, pepper and mint and remove from the heat.

Brush the fruit liberally with the sauce and serve with assorted white cheeses.

Serves 6

A SOUTHERN EUROPEAN SUMMER
DELICACY

8   large fresh figs
    black pepper
½   lime
2 tbsp   yogurt
2   blood oranges, sliced

This one may be new to you, but try it. I guarantee you will enjoy. Figs are readily found at any European green grocer.

Cut the figs in half lengthwise and place the halves, meat side down, on the barbecue. Grill over a medium to high heat (350 to 400°F) for approximately 2 minutes.

Turn the figs over and sprinkle with the black pepper and grill for 1 minute more.

Squeeze the lime juice over the top of the figs. Dab each one with ¼ tbsp of yogurt. Close the lid, shut off the heat and allow to stand for 30 to 40 seconds.

Remove and serve with fresh slices of blood orange.

Serves 4

BANANAS

IN A RUM SAUCE

*This dessert will top
off any dinner
year-round.*

3	large bananas
¼ cup	butter
1 cup	Demerara brown sugar
⅓ cup	banana liqueur
¼ tsp	cinnamon powder
⅓ cup	dark rum
2 tbsp	butter, melted
1 tbsp	olive oil
	vanilla ice cream

Prepare the sauce by melting the ¼ cup of butter in a saucepan. Stir in the brown sugar, banana liqueur and cinnamon. Cook and stir over a low to medium heat until all the sugar has dissolved. Add the rum and simmer for 3 minutes to release the alcohol but retain the flavours. Remove from the heat and allow to stand at room or outside temperature.

Combine the melted butter and olive oil in a small dish. Peel the bananas, brush lightly with the butter mixture and place on the grid of a barbecue preheated to 300°F. Using the indirect method of cooking, barbecue the bananas on the unfired area of the grid for 8 to 10 minutes, just to heat them through.

Gently move the bananas directly over the heat and grill until they are very lightly charred. Gently turn and baste with the melted butter mixture during this cooking period.

While the bananas are cooking place a medium-sized scoop of ice cream into each of four dessert bowls.

Gently transfer the bananas to a cutting board and slice crosswise into ⅜-inch rounds. Arrange equal amounts over and around each scoop of ice cream.

Bring the rum sauce to a just-heated stage and drizzle equal amounts around each scoop of ice cream.

Serves 4

Index

Indicates a recipe barbecued low and slow.

Addresses

Barbecue Manufacturers

A good website is
barbecuen.com/gas-manf.htm

Binford Barbecues
218 Riverview Park
Calgary, AL
T2C 4A1

The Brinkman Corporation
4215 McEwen Rd.
Dallas, TX
75244

The Ducane Company
800 Dutch Square Blvd., Suite 20
Columbia, SC
29210

Grillmaster
6324 NW 72nd Ave.
Miami, FL
33166

The Holland Grill Company Inc.
600 Irving Parkway
Hollysprings, NC
27540

Klose Construction and Fabrication
2214½ West 34th St.
Houston, TX
77018

Napoleon Appliance Corporation
214 Bayview Drive
Barrie, ON
L4N 4Y8

Pitt's and Spitt's
14221 Eastex Freeway
Houston, TX
77032

Traeger Industries Inc.
PO Box 829
Mt. Angel, OR
97362

Weber Barbecues
200 East Daniels Rd.
Palatine, IL
60067–6266

Spices and Foods

Pappy's Choice Seasonings
PO Box 5257
Fresno, CA
93755

Pendery's Inc.
1221 Manufacturing St.
Dallas, TX
75207

Timber Crest Farms
(Sonoma brand)
4791 Dry Creek Rd.
Healdsburg, CA
95448

Hills Foods
(Game and exotic meats)
109–3650 Bonneville Pl.
Burnaby, BC
V3N 4T7

The Best Little Pork Shoppe
167 Huron Rd. E.
Shakespeare, ON
N0B 2P0